NOV 13

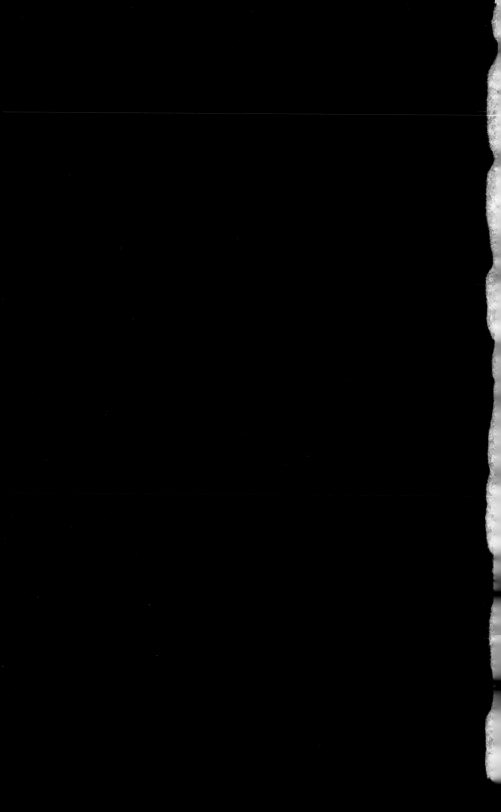

LOOKING FOR STRANGERS

Looking for Strangers

The True Story of My Hidden Wartime Childhood

Dori Katz

THE UNIVERSITY OF CHICAGO PRESS   *Chicago & London*

DORI KATZ is professor emeritus of modern languages and literature at Trinity College. She is the author of *Hiding in Other People's Houses.*

The University of Chicago Press, Chicago 60637
The University of Chicago Press, Ltd., London
© 2013 by The University of Chicago
All rights reserved. Published 2013.
Printed in the United States of America

22 21 20 19 18 17 16 15 14 13   1 2 3 4 5

ISBN-13: 978-0-226-05862-7 (cloth)
ISBN-13: 978-0-226-06333-1 (e-book)
DOI: 10.7208/chicago/9780226063331.001.0001

Library of Congress Cataloging-in-Publication Data

Katz, Dori, author.
  Looking for strangers: the true story of my hidden wartime childhood / Dori Katz.
    pages cm
    ISBN 978-0-226-05862-7 (cloth: alkaline paper)—ISBN 978-0-226-06333-1 (e-book)
  1. Katz, Dori. 2. Hidden children (Holocaust)—Belgium—Biography. 3. Jews—Belgium—Biography. I. Title.
    D804.48.K314 2013
    940.53′18092—dc23
    [B]   2013003400

♾ This paper meets the requirements of ANSI/NISO Z39.48-1992 (Permanence of Paper).

For my father, Moishe Chaim Katz, 1910–1945

For my mother, Goldie Dychtwald Katz, 1913–2003

Since you won't budge, I am the one who must go back
after so many years to those deserted streets,
find your house, knock on the door and ask to be taken in.

DORI KATZ, *Hiding in Other People's Houses*

CONTENTS

I was born in Antwerp in 1939, one year before the Germans occupied Belgium in World War II. My mother—who was originally from Jeżów, a small town in Poland—came to Belgium by herself, to be with her brother in 1934. My father had come a year earlier from Svalava, Czechoslovakia, with his family; he was one of seven siblings. My mother and father met in Antwerp and married in 1938.

Once the persecution of the Jews started, relatives, siblings, parents, and friends began to disappear. My father was arrested in September 1942 and deported to Auschwitz. Five months later I was placed in hiding with a Belgian Catholic family in Beersel, which is only seven miles from Brussels, but to me, at the age of three, it was a very distant world. My mother survived alone in Brussels with the help of counterfeit papers that gave her a new name, a Belgian identity, and a Christian religion. We were reunited in 1944 for a few months, but then, on January 16, 1945, my mother placed me in an orphanage in the town of La Hulpe, twelve miles from Brussels, for two years. In 1952 my mother and I left Brussels and settled in California.

The parts of this memoir relating to Poland in the 1930s and Belgium in the 1940s are based on the stories my mother told me, over and over, about her life. As we both grew older, I began to take notes whenever she would talk about those times, first out of curiosity, then thinking that someday I might write about them. Whenever I went to Israel to visit my uncle Benjamin, who survived Auschwitz, he would reminisce about his youth in Antwerp and his role in my parents' courtship; his stories also informed those parts of the book. The chapter dealing with me as a hidden child at the age of three and a half is based on my own fragmented but sharp memories, which were corroborated forty years later by Jeanne Walschot, who was fourteen years old when I came to live with her family.

INTRODUCTION

I knew it was my mother when the telephone rang that morning, not only because she always called me around that time on Sundays, but also because I thought the ring sounded angry and reproachful.

"So, you're really going to Belgium," she said, wasting no time for introductory niceties when I picked up the phone.

"Hi, Mom, fine—thanks, and you?" I answered, and then told her that I hadn't changed my mind. She repeated all the objections she had already voiced when I stated my intentions to search for the strangers who had hidden me during the war. She reminded me that it had been over forty years ago. "You were a child then; for you, it was nothing," she told me. "You can't possibly remember anything about that time; those people did it for money. What makes you think they'll be glad to see you? Besides, they're probably dead by now."

"I don't care," I replied. "I want to find out. I'm going."

"Why are you doing this?" she asked again.

It was hard to answer, since I couldn't even articulate to myself why the compelling need, decades after the war, to recover memories of my life between the ages of three and seven, the years of our separation.

"What do you want to find out? Just ask me," she said. "Do you know how difficult it was for me to give you up, how much I suffered, always worrying if you were safe? You were just a child—you didn't understand."

I told her that was not the point, that this was not a criticism of her as a mother. But we couldn't understand each other. I couldn't figure out why my projected trip was so painful to her, and she couldn't believe that I needed to reconnect with a past that excluded her.

As we talked, I pictured her in her housedress, sitting on her plastic-covered couch, the shades of the living room drawn against the midday California sun, her wig perched on the black vase on the dresser (she always took it off when she was alone). The table would be set, ready for the big meal she would serve at noon to her boyfriend when he came by to spend the day. She often called me when everything was prepared, the unmolded apple-lime Jell-O ring wiggling on the kitchen counter, the codfish steaks ready to go under the broiler, the soup simmering on the stove. She probably had her slippered feet up on the glass coffee table, waiting for him, leaving enough time to change housedresses, then put on a little makeup and her wig.

I didn't think she would tell him about our conversation; this was just between the two of us. Suddenly I wished I were there, sitting safely at the kitchen table with her, with no tension between us. We had lived on different coasts for decades now and only saw each other twice a year; these weekly telephone calls were like an umbilical cord still connecting us after all that time apart.

She didn't wish me a happy birthday, although I knew she hadn't forgotten. It was the first time that she hadn't sent me a gift or a card with money for the occasion. I always felt a little uncomfortable taking money from her at my age, especially since I knew that I earned so much more as a college professor than she did as a seamstress, but I saw these gifts as tokens of her love, and so I accepted the cash or the inevitable flannel pajamas gratefully.

Nor did she wish me a good trip but instead hung up as I tried once again to justify my need to go to Belgium: She and I had never talked about the unshared years of my childhood, maybe because they had been too painful for her. For me, they had not seemed important until lately. Perhaps because I was now in my mid-forties and knowing that I would never have a child, I wanted to retrieve the child I had been. Or perhaps I was like many people who have gone through a traumatic experience but do not speak of it until decades later.

I knew the facts: My mother and I had been separated during World War II and reunited for a few months when the Allies landed in Normandy; then we were separated again as the war continued and finally reunited for good sometime after the peace. I barely remembered those years, and my fragmented memories were like clouds constantly drifting, dissipating, and re-forming.

Who were the strangers who had taken me in? Were they still there in the same Belgian village? Why did they take such a risk? How could I thank them? Had they loved me, and had I loved them? What had I been like as a child? And then there was the mystery of my father: What had happened to him after his arrest in 1942? All my mother and I knew is that he had been deported to Auschwitz and never came back. My mother thought what had happened was clear enough, but I needed to know more; I wanted to find out about his life there and about his death. I had learned recently that there were war archives about Jews in Brussels in a government building; perhaps I would find answers there. In spite of my mother's disapproval, I was going to go to Belgium—albeit with more trepidation than eagerness.

AS IF IT WERE YESTERDAY, 1982

It all started with watching a movie about my own life playing at noon in a movie theater in midtown Manhattan. Usually I love going to the movies midday by myself even when the sun is out; I enjoy the solitary escape into a cave of shadows that transports you to another half-world so that you come out afterward blinking in the daylight, disoriented as if you were coming back from a faraway place. But this time, I walked around the block three times before making up my mind to go inside the theater to see the documentary *As If It Were Yesterday*.

The box office was open and there was no one in line, but I couldn't bring myself to buy a ticket; I kept walking around the block. I was reluctant to enter the theater, fearing perhaps that the film would touch a nerve and release a flood of painful memories. More likely, I was afraid of being disappointed, of learning nothing, of being irritated by another pointless, sugarcoated, sentimental treatment of the Holocaust. It was with this anxiety that I finally rushed into the theater two minutes before showtime.

There were only three other people in the auditorium. I thought the theater manager would decide it was not worthwhile to screen the film, but the theater curtains parted, and from the moment the Neige piano music started, I sat transfixed and would be for the next hour and a half. On the screen, two white-haired women appeared, talking in Flemish, about little Miriam, their neighbors' daughter. It was 1942; Belgium had been occupied by the Germans for two years. The child was out on an errand, or perhaps she was at school, when the women heard the Gestapo come and arrest her family. Maybe the Gestapo men didn't know there was also a little girl in the family. In any case, the parents said nothing about her as they were herded into the van waiting outside.

When little Miriam came back, the two women recounted, they "just couldn't let her walk into that empty apartment all by herself; she was just a little girl." They decided to take in the child until relatives would claim her, but no one ever came for her, so they kept her throughout the war. No one in the building said anything. When the war was over, Miriam's parents did not return, and she continued to live with the women and became "their" daughter.

The film continued along those lines: A schoolteacher who was told that the parents of her two Jewish pupils had just been arrested took them home with her, then later found them a safe hiding place and went to see them every week to make sure they were all right. A nurse smuggled a child into a sickroom. A doctor hid a dozen children in his clinic for tuberculosis, and a radiologist helped him by faking X-rays, which were used to safeguard the children. A priest hid children in his cellar. A shoemaker saw a friend being arrested on the street and, feeling sorry for the man's son, took him in. More and more people told their story in Flemish and in French, in a casual way, as though saving Jewish children from the Gestapo were a mundane, ordinary activity.

Some people were bystanders who felt compelled to react to what they had witnessed. "It was natural" was a phrase often heard in the documentary. "You just couldn't let that little child be taken, or abandoned, or go into an empty house when you knew the parents had been arrested."

Others joined clandestine organizations and sought out children to save and people who would hide them, or looked for safe convents, homes, or asylums—places into which children could "disappear."

"Because," the rescuers said, "it was a way of protesting what was happening in our country." Rescuing these children made them feel less helpless in the face of the occupation, but mostly they did it because, as they insisted: "You don't kill children. It isn't right."

A white-haired woman with tinted glasses, identified as Andrée Guelin, explained the networks that were set up to save the children. She told of the participation of various resistance and underground groups, the money that changed hands, the contacts, and the little notebooks with coded numbers standing for the children and the coded places they were hidden, so that no names would be revealed should these notebooks have fallen into the wrong hands. She also spoke of how painful it was to take the children from the parents, how sad everyone was, how frightened at the separation and of the uncertainty of the future. For many families, it would be the last time they saw one another.

I had also been hidden as a child, starting in 1943. Forgetting that I had not been interviewed for the film, my heart began to race when photographs of the children then and now started to appear: What if one of those photos was of me? Were any of these people speaking about me? Had they been the ones to save me? I don't know if I wished for or dreaded the possibility.

This was the very first time I had seen any documentation about children with my Holocaust experience. The term "hidden child" hadn't been coined yet, and there had been little written about the experiences of those young survivors.

I walked out of the theater very shaken, suddenly overwhelmed by the need to find the people who had hidden me. I wanted to reconnect with them, to embrace them, to thank them. I had been so young during the war that my memories were vague, yet some images of separation and loss had remained very sharp in my mind. The film brought validation for those hazy, buried memories. What I half remembered had really happened; I hadn't simply imagined those terrible years.

Now I knew I wasn't the only one who had experienced this "hiding." I felt a sort of kinship with those other children, now grown-up, who had been saved from German extermination. I also felt awed, suddenly aware of all the work, the planning, and the risks taken by strangers just to save someone like me—a child of people who were not important, not rich, influential, or political. People like my father, a Czech shoe store owner, and my mother, his Polish wife, both of them living with their little daughter in Brussels—ordinary people sought out by strangers from a country they had never set foot in, to be killed for no other reason other than their being Jewish. I had to find the people who hid me; it would let me feel like I was saving something from loss, forty years after the event.

Back in Hartford, Connecticut, teaching my classes at Trinity College, I could not get *As If It Were Yesterday* out of my mind. I spent the next few weeks trying to contact the two filmmakers. I had learned from the *New York Times* review that they were in the city to publicize their documentary. After a few false leads and many phone calls, I reached them and we talked for a long time. They seemed eager to meet me, especially after I sent them some of my poetry dealing with my childhood. We chose a date, and I took a bus from Hartford to meet them in a coffee shop in midtown Manhattan.

The filmmakers were younger than I expected; I had assumed that they must have lived through the war themselves in order to make such a film. But that was not the case: they were born after the war. But both were children of survivors. Myriam, whose parents had been in hiding during the war, was of Belgian origin, like me, while Esther was born in Germany to a Jewish father and a Catholic mother.

I told them my story.

"For you, it was nothing; you were only a child. You didn't suffer. You don't even remember." Those were the words, I told them, that I heard all the time from my mother when she referred to our experience in Belgium during the war. She would talk about her difficult times after my father was arrested by the Gestapo, alluding to all the things she had to do in order to survive. She told me how hard it had been for her to put me in the hands of strangers she had never seen before who were going to place me with a Belgian Catholic family for my own safety. For a long time, she did not know where I was.

She had needed much strength and forbearance to go on after her beloved brother and his family were deported and as all her friends and relatives disappeared, one by one. But she wouldn't let me speak to her about what it had been like for me, separated from her and my father, living with strangers. She kept telling me that because I had been so young, what happened had not affected me and therefore could not be important.

In truth, I did not recall having suffered, although I remembered more than my mother would admit. But my memories were so vague and fragmented that they were easily dismissed as childish inventions; I myself did not trust them. And that they were inconsequential was easy to accept since compared to my mother's friends' stories, they seemed rather benign.

In Belgium after the war and, later, in Los Angeles, where my mother and I wound up in 1952, her friends were all European Jews— therefore "survivors," a term coined by Terrence Des Pres in his seminal book, *The Survivors*, and quickly adopted by those who had lived through the Holocaust and experienced the horrors of concentration camp life. I certainly didn't identify myself as one of them; my own story paled in comparison to the hardships they had endured. I had not been starved, beaten, tortured, experimented on, or suffered other such horrors. It would have seemed strangely presumptuous for me to claim kinship.

After the war, I remember yearning for my father as a child. Since my mother and I never knew how or when he died in Auschwitz, I used to have fantasies of him turning up, unexpectedly, and recognizing us. We would be a complete family again, like those of my childhood friends in Belgium in the 1940s. For a long time I had little thought of the family who had hidden me for a year and a half, from 1943 to mid-1944. Even though I remembered my first meeting with them, which entailed separating from my mother, I had no recollection of my last days in their home or of leaving them. My mother, who met them when she came to take me back, refused to talk about that meeting and would always answer any of my questions with "What do you want to know for?"

The filmmakers Esther and Myriam asked if I'd ever seen the Belgian family again after the war, despite my mother's feelings. I hadn't, I told them, but I thought about them a great deal throughout the years. Perhaps not at first, not right after leaving them, when for some reason I didn't live with my mother for two years but was placed in an institution for homeless children in La Hulpe, Belgium. I remember being with my mother for a short time, perhaps a few months or so after leaving the Catholic family in the summer of 1944. It was so cold that December, we walked with socks over our shoes to avoid falling on the slippery sidewalks. But in January 1945, I wound up in the orphanage for almost two years. I never knew why.

After leaving La Hulpe at age seven and a half, I was so happy when my mother and I were finally reunited in Brussels that I don't remember thinking of that Belgian family. I had to adjust to a French school while my primary language was Flemish. I was placed in the third grade, where I was academically behind the other students. I had a lot of catching up to do, but I made friends among my classmates and started a new life. Five years later, my mother and I came to America, and there was yet another language to learn, a new school to blend into, and a new life to adopt.

Years later, when I was pretty well Americanized and in college, I started thinking about the family that hid me; I drew a blank. What was their surname? What village were they from? All I remembered were a few names like Mama Gine, which was what I called the middle-aged woman who replaced my mother; Papa Franz, her husband; and Jeanne, their teenage daughter.

I went on to tell Myriam and Esther that my mother claimed she didn't remember their names either; she was also vague about the village they had lived in. Pronouncing it differently each time, she would pull out the name of a place but had no idea of how to spell it. I had tried various spellings myself and looked them up on a map of Belgium—but no luck.

My mother had had no earlier relationship with the people who hid me and had met them only that one time when she came to fetch me; she had never wanted to see them again afterward. Even now I don't really know why, but I can only guess that those were such difficult and painful times for her that she hated anything connected with them. She refused to acknowledge our debt to that family. She insisted on seeing their role as a commercial one because they did take money. Yes, they were paid a monthly sum for my upkeep by the White Brigade, the resistance group that had organized my hiding. But she would not recognize the enormous risk that the family had run.

Perhaps she was never comfortable with the fact that she had given up her daughter, even though it was to save me. Maybe that's why she had never been able to accept the notion that I had also suffered during the war years and that she had been unable to do anything to prevent it. She always repeated her standard remark about my experience: "You were only three then; you can't remember."

For many years, I thought so too, but after seeing *As If It Were Yesterday*, I knew it wasn't true. My father's sudden disappearance, the separation first from my mother, then from the Flemish family I had become attached to, my misery in the La Hulpe institute—you don't forget such loss and upheavals, even if you only half remember them. I told Esther and Myriam that their film had opened the floodgates of yearning for me.

Now I realized that the more I knew about those years, the easier it would be to escape the feeling of being haunted by them. I wanted to bring everything into the open, to dispel the shadows, to have a grasp on that foggy childhood so that I could stop looking for it. But I didn't know where or how to start.

Myriam and Esther were surprised that I didn't know about the archives in Brussels. After the war, the Red Cross had turned over to the Belgian authorities all the documents pertaining to Jews living in their country during those years. There was a file for every person who had been there—there would be one for my father, one for my mother, and even one for me, just a year old when the Germans invaded Belgium.

To complete these holdings, the various resistance and underground groups that helped hide or smuggle Jews out of danger had turned over their files. A certain Madame Aubrey was in charge of the archives at the Ministry of Public Health in Brussels; she could put various materials together for me. My file would have the name of the people who hid me, their address at the time, and other pertinent information. I might also find out what had happened to my father after he was arrested; all I knew was that he had died in Auschwitz.

Esther was going to Brussels in a few days and would look at the archives for me. I didn't put much stock in her confidence that she would find information on my family; it couldn't be that easy. I tried to forget her promise. But a few weeks later, I received a letter from her saying that the information I sought was indeed in the Ministry of Public Health. I had been hidden by Franz and Régine Walschot, 170 chaussée d'Uccle, in the village of Beersel. My "war" name had been Astrid Von der Laar. Later I was sent to an institution called L'Oeuvre Royale du Grand Air pour les Petits à la Hulpe.

There was also a whole file on my father: He had been deported from Malines on Convoy No. 9 on September 12, 1942, two days after his arrest; his Auschwitz camp number was 177679. Esther added that there was much more information but that I should come to Brussels and read the files myself.

I was stunned. All those years of my questioning fragmentary memories, and the answers were in files in an office in Brussels all this time. At first, I couldn't believe what Esther was telling me and thought she was playing a cruel joke on me; I felt hurt by her macabre sense of humor. But then I realized that could not the case because some of her revelations were not new to me. I had been registered as Astrid at my birth in Antwerp, and it was what I had been called in Belgium by everyone except my mother. It had been my first name until I legally reclaimed Dori when I became a naturalized American citizen at the age of eighteen in California.

I called my mother in Los Angeles and told her about the information in Esther's letter. Initially, she was noncommittal. "Perhaps," she said, and then added that it was indeed my father's camp number but that she didn't remember how she knew this.

Then she asked why I was bothering with all this, why after so many years did I want to find out what was no longer important? Why did I want to revisit those years? There was no need for it.

I couldn't explain to her why it was so important to me. All I knew was my excitement at the idea of contacting the people who had hidden me. For once, my mother's attitude did not dampen my enthusiasm. Though I was still not convinced I would find the Walschots, I began thinking that I would try. I let my mother change the subject.

After our call ended, I took out the photographs I had of the Belgian family and me that had been taken during the war. One photograph in particular interested me. It showed a rather heavy woman in her fifties, Mama Gine; a man, also in his fifties, with white hair and a dashing mustache, Papa Franz; a child holding on to his arm (me); and a young girl of about fourteen, Jeanne, in a pretty white dress. We were standing in front of a stone house. It was a picture I knew by heart since I had looked at it many times trying to jog my memory, yet I had never noticed the number of the house above the front door although it was clearly legible: 170, the same number that Esther had told me was the Walschots' address. I decided then to go back to Belgium.

JEŻÓW, 1918

My mother, Golda Dychtwald, was five years old when she developed a rash on her head. No one noticed this at first. Aurelia, her own mother, had died of typhus when Golda was still an infant, and her stepmother, Esther—who was pregnant for the second time in two years—was too ill to pay attention to much else other than her own nausea and fatigue. Her first pregnancy had ended in a stillbirth, and Esther worried that it would be the same with this one.

Golda's father did not pay much attention to her condition, either. Things were not going well. He worked all day tutoring unwilling and dull-witted boys in Hebrew and the Torah so that they could assume their place in the Polish village, the shtetl of Jeżów, by being bar mitzvahed. His role as a teacher, a rebbe, was too prestigious an occupation for him to easily supplement his meager income by doing odd jobs, but his salary was not enough to feed five—soon to be six—people, which included the three children from his first marriage. They would have been even worse off had it not been for the handouts that they received from the Zelmans, his deceased first wife's parents, who were well-to-do merchants in Skierniewice, a town not far from the shtetl. His former in-laws saw their grand-children Fischel, Henna, and Golda on all religious holidays and remembered their birthdays with cash gifts, which were usually spent on food or books for the rebbe's library, important as that was to him.

My mother didn't particularly feel loved or spoiled by her grandparents, two bitter old people, she told me, who constantly complained about the cost of everything. In fact, she still bore them a grudge many years later. "They could have done something about my head," she would tell me. "They had the money, but they were too stingy even with their granddaughter."

So at first, Golda's father did not notice her rash, and when he did, he believed his wife, who said that it was nothing, just one of those things children always get, and if it didn't clear up soon, they would have the midwife look at it.

There were no doctors in Jeżów in 1918. If you got sick enough to really need one, you would go to Lodz or Skierniewice, the two nearest cities. But such trips and consultations were expensive and undertaken only as a last resort. Most diseases seemed to cure themselves, or it might be that the sick got used to their maladies and other people grew accustomed to seeing them ill. No one thought it odd if some people always seemed to be coughing, scratching, shaking, or short of breath.

When the midwife was consulted, she could brew special teas, disinfect a wound, bandage a cut, apply leeches for bleeding (which was thought to be a cure for most ailments), and make most pains go away by giving you something to eat, drink, or smell.

It is hard for me to imagine what life could have been like for my mother as a child since I spent most of my life in big cities: Brussels, San Francisco, Los Angeles, Hartford, New York. But when my mother was growing up, Jeżów was a small town, twenty-one miles south of Lodz, one of the biggest cities in Poland. A history of the town reports that in 1920 there were 1,048 Jews living there and that in 1923, when my mother was ten years old, Jeżów was subjected to a violent anti-Semitic pogrom: Poles raced through the neighborhood, burning homes, destroying shops, and beating up people in the streets. Although my mother doesn't remember this, it probably instilled in her a strong distrust of non-Jews throughout her life; deep down they were always out to harm Jews no matter how they behaved. She evidently retained this suspicion even for the Catholic family that hid me during the war.

But in 1918, in spite of the midwife ministries, my mother's rash did not go away. It turned into scabs, especially on her scalp, and those scabs became infected, oozing a yellowish-red pus. The midwife who was called in applied a dressing on the sores; they dried up but left big red scars, more like welts, all over Golda's head. They were not supposed to hurt or itch, but Golda was always scratching herself, which inflamed the welts.

Esther, who had by then given birth to a sickly boy, was forever telling Golda to stop scratching, that she was only making matters worse. At school the teacher told Golda to ask her parents to take her to a doctor, but Esther felt she couldn't leave the baby, and she refused her husband's offer to watch him, citing all the work to be done and the endless meals she had to prepare.

My mother's father was not an easy man to cook for. Not because he was finicky but because he had no teeth, so he was only able to eat soft foods. The loss of his teeth had not been an accident, nor had it been due to illness; it had been his way of avoiding being drafted into the Polish army. The recruiters had come to Jeżów one day and announced that it was time for Jewish bums to stop living off the sweat of Polish citizens and do their share by joining the army. All men over sixteen were required to register for the draft the next day at the synagogue, and some would be enlisted on the spot.

My grandfather was petrified; stories circulating about the treatment of Jews in the army were frightening: Jews were beaten by the other soldiers and given the dirtiest, hardest tasks. Worst of all, they were shipped far away from their villages and often never heard from again.

He worried who would take care of his wife and child. Even though he was only twenty-two at the time, he was already married and a father. Then he remembered the rumors he had heard about certain physical defects that could keep you out of the army. They wouldn't take cripples, or men with bad feet or a broken hand, or those without teeth. The latter seemed the easiest way out. So that night, my grandfather went to the local butcher's house and asked him to pull all his teeth out. Whether that or something else ended up keeping him out of the army, my grandfather was never to know; but they didn't enlist him the next day when they took some of the other men of Jeżów.

Of course, my grandfather had intended to get dentures, but they were very expensive, something to be saved up for. He knew his first wife's parents wouldn't pay for them, and his own parents had been dead for years; they would have been too poor, anyway. So my grandfather tried to save up, but whenever he had a little money set aside, something else came up—like the birth of his second child, Henna; and the third, my mother; then his first wife's illness and death; and his second marriage to Esther. One needed money to remarry.

So my grandfather became used to not having any teeth. Like the other people of Jeżów who, although not happy about their afflictions, no longer fought against them, he stopped thinking about it. I can picture my grandfather at twenty-five, a young yeshiva student rebbe who looked older than his rabbi because of the sunken cheeks in his bearded face. It must have affected his speech, too, making him talk like an old man.

"Oh, no, he was very handsome, my father, in spite of it. I wish I had a picture to show you," my mother told me many years later. "But I have none—none of my father or my mother or my grandparents. You know, in those days, people didn't walk around with cameras all the time, snapping pictures. You had your picture taken on special occasions, like bar mitzvahs or weddings. When I left Poland, I didn't think of taking any of those along. Who knew then that I would never see my family again? Who knew that there would be a Hitler?"

Although it was hard for me to imagine my toothless grandfather, Chaim Dychtwald, as handsome, when I looked at my mother, I could believe it. Where else would she have gotten those high cheekbones, those dark, lively eyes and tawny skin? Besides, I like the fact that my mother, cynical and bitter about most things, should remember her father as handsome.

But in 1918 my grandfather regretted that he had stopped saving money for his dentures because he would have gladly spent whatever money he had accumulated on a doctor for his daughter Golda. In the end, no one took her to a doctor. Fischel, Golda's older brother, was apprenticed with an uncle in Lodz at a shoe factory. He was sixteen and, having discovered girls, came home to the shtetl of Jeżów less and less often. Henna, Golda's older sister, was only ten and was sympathetic but, at the same time, repulsed by her younger sister's skin disease.

Eventually Golda's welts stopped swelling and itching, but now every time she put her hand in her hair, great chunks of it came out, and bald patches began to appear on her scalp.

"It's nothing," said the midwife, when she was once again consulted. "It's just old, diseased hair. She's only a child; it will grow back." But it got worse, and little by little, Golda was going bald.

Esther kept her out of school. She had given birth for the second time and was pregnant again. Even though Golda was then only seven, she could help her stepmother around the house by watching the baby, bringing water from the well, washing the vegetables, and doing many other small necessary daily tasks. School had been an ordeal for her because the other children made fun of her, mocking her appearance mimicking her relentless scratching. She missed so many classes that she was always behind in her lessons. Her teacher thought she was dumb and had told her as much so many times that my mother began to believe that there was something wrong with her, with her head—the source of all her grief.

All my life I had heard my mother rationalize her failings because of her "head." When she had trouble learning to read English in Los Angeles or when I couldn't teach her new vocabulary, she would say, tapping her head: "There is something wrong there; I just can't learn anything. Just doesn't go in." Strange that my mother should equate her lack of hair with a lack of cognitive power, yet there were some things she simply could not learn. Looking back on it, I think today we would probably say that she had a learning disability, but this was not something that was recognized in Poland during her childhood nor in Belgium or California when I was growing up.

Soon Golda was kept out of school altogether. She had disliked school because she was made to feel ugly and stupid there, but she did not like staying at home, either. Her stepmother seemed to always be after her with some job that needed to be done.

Golda was lonely: Her half-brothers were too young for companionship; meanwhile her older brother was living in Lodz, and Henna was in school all day. She also sensed that she was missing out on something; when she played with other children, they seemed to know many things that she didn't. They referred to things she had never heard of, used words she didn't understand. After a while, she asked to be sent back to school, but her stepmother had gotten used to having her around and was too dependent on her to let her go. Once again, Esther was sick during another pregnancy.

"Do you know," my mother said when she was telling me the story of her childhood, "that I don't even remember the names of any of the children my stepmother had. There were seven of them, but I think that three died before they were five. The others Hitler got, along with my stepmother, may she rest in peace. I only remember her being pregnant or with a child at her breast. Poor woman, she did not have an easy life . . . but I really don't remember any of the names."

The only good thing about being kept at home was that Golda was able to spend time with her father. He, who valued learning above everything else, did not want her to be illiterate and taught her himself. At home, with no one taunting her and with her father's encouragement, Golda learned how to read and write Yiddish. She read some of the books on his shelves and eavesdropped when he was preparing boys for their bar mitzvahs; in fact, she was far from ignorant for a girl her age and knew more of the Torah and Talmud than most other children did, including her father's students. This probably explains my mother's attitude about books; while there were none in our apartment in Brussels when I was growing up— my mother never learned to read and write Flemish or French well, or later English for that matter—she was very supportive of my interest in reading, which I satisfied by spending long afternoons at the public library not far from our house. Although she said she herself had no time for such frivolities, she was proud of the prizes I earned for my performance in school. Perhaps my own love of books and later my career as a professor of literature is connected to my grandfather's profession, which my mother admired.

As for my mother's skin condition, it never cleared up. Everyone in the shtetl had gotten so used to it that they no longer thought it strange that she had welts and bald spots on her scalp. Eventually the welts disappeared, but the baldness remained. Her condition had endured for so long that people seemed not to notice her baldness anymore, just as they stopped asking my grandfather when he was going to get dentures or telling the butcher that he should take care of his cough. But my mother did not accept her condition. By combing the little hair she had left back a certain way and wearing scarves, she was able to cleverly hide the baldness. I think she was a very pretty child, but she continued to suffer from the humiliation of not having much hair all her life and never gave up looking for the right doctor who could find a cure for her baldness.

I remember as a child of eight in Belgium after the war stopping with her in front of every pharmacy display hawking remedies claiming to cure baldness. I had to read labels of all the lotions and creams on store shelves that promised gorgeous hair within weeks and to translate them from French into Flemish or Yiddish for her. Later, after we immigrated to America—to California, the land of dreams, of movie stars' hair—it was from English into Yiddish. She would find advertisements in newspapers and magazines, and hear about products hawked on television and the radio, and I would call the numbers listed or write to the manufacturer or ask bewildered salesclerks if the stuff "really worked."

My mother always felt like an outsider because of her lack of hair, in school in her home town of Jeżów, Poland; and in Antwerp, Belgium, when she was a young woman dating and part of a large group of friends. She felt like she stood apart and worried that someone would figure out her "handicap." It didn't prevent her from having boyfriends and eventually marrying, but feeling apart from the group made her a nonconformist. I sometimes think that this lack of solidarity with others served her well during the war. She had never quite played by the rules because she felt that rules didn't apply to her since she was an outsider. When Antwerp and Brussels were occupied during the war, she didn't always obey the racial laws. At times, for example, she wouldn't wear the yellow star that identified her as a Jew. She didn't report her earnings as a cleaning lady to the Association of Jews in Belgium, an infraction punishable by arrest; when she registered with the agency, she gave a false address. I realize that her survival, and therefore mine, depended mostly on luck, but I can't help thinking that her rebelliousness played a part in it.

My mother, who made heads turn in Antwerp and Brussels as a young woman and even in Los Angeles, when she was no longer so young, never believed in her own beauty, in her pluck, in her strength. Her baldness was the dark center of her life. No man could really love her because of it, she said, admitting my father had, but that he was "an exception."

"I never remarried because of that. I knew that if I told a man about that, he wouldn't want to marry me anymore." Years after the war, one engagement after another was broken, and she always blamed it on her baldness, no matter what the reason was. I had barely gotten used to her newest boyfriend when he disappeared from our lives, sometimes to my ambivalent chagrin. On the one hand, I wanted to be part of a conventional family: mother, father, and child. On the other hand, I always saw a potential husband for my mother as a competitor for her love and was afraid that I would be sent away again as I had been to La Hulpe—neither ever happened.

"He said he didn't want to be stuck with a woman who had a child," she would say when the relationship ended, "but that is just an excuse. I know the real reason." Or of another breakup she would explain: "He wants a woman who will go live with him in Israel, which I won't do. But I know that's not the reason he doesn't want to marry me."

In 1927, when my mother was fourteen years old, she went to Skier-niewice, to live with her brother Fischel, who was eleven years older than her and married with two children. "I wanted to get out of the house. I really didn't get along with my stepmother because she was always after me with some job when I wanted to go out with friends; besides Skierniewice was a city, which was better than Jeżów, the shtetl we were living in. But in truth, I went because Fischel had promised to take me to a doctor for my hair," she once told me.

At Fischel's, she helped around the house, took care of the chil-dren. "I was my sister-in-law's servant. But I loved my brother, except that he didn't keep his promise," she told me. "Today I can't hold this against him considering what happened to him and his family."

When she was sixteen, my mother moved out of her brother's house and got an apartment of her own. She worked mostly as a maid, cleaning lady, or taking care of strangers' children. "I didn't make much money, but I ate my meals at my older sister Henna's house," she explained. "She was married by then and also living in Skierniewice. Sometimes, I would go to dinner at my brother's, but his wife always made me feel as though I was taking food out of her mouth, so I stopped going there. Of course, on Shabbat, I always ate at my grandparents' house; it wasn't an easy life, but I was young and I liked being on my own."

Then in 1930 her brother left Poland with his wife and children, and settled in Antwerp; he began writing home that life was much easier for Jews in Belgium, jobs more plentiful, and that they should all come. Of course, no one in Golda's family would consider it. The Zelmans, their grandparents, were too old to emigrate; Henna's husband did not want to leave his parents; and Chaim, Golda's father, could not come with all his brood and his forever-pregnant wife. But my mother wanted to go; she became obsessed with the idea of leaving Poland, just as before she had been driven by the wish to leave Jeżów.

"There is nothing here for me," she kept telling everyone. "I can make a life out there. Fischel will take care of me. He'll watch over me, don't worry," she told her grandparents, and begged them to give her the money—as with everything else, it was a question of money. "You owe it to me, I said to my grandmother," my mother told me years later. "I kept reminding her that it was her fault that I was bald, that she didn't take me to the doctor in time, that her dead daughter, my mother, would have been very upset with her. I just kept on harping on the subject, bringing it up all the time, so that in the end my grandparents gave me the money.

"When it came time to leave, my father was very upset," my mother went on. "He was so worried about me. I remember he cried when I went to say good-bye to him. He kept on telling me that he knew he would never see me again. Poor man, he was right; we never did see each other again. Who could have known that those terrible things were going to happen? My only consolation is that my father did not die in a concentration camp but died in 1939—in fact, a couple of days before you were born. They kept the news from me, afraid, I suppose, that I would be so upset that I would miscarry; it's never good to mix death with birth. I thought something was wrong when Fischel didn't come to the hospital to see his niece. I just couldn't understand why my beloved brother didn't just rush right over to take a look at you. Of course, he couldn't, he was sitting shivah, mourning our father's death, as was the custom, and couldn't leave the house for seven days.

"I don't know what my father died of," my mother continued. "He was sick. His life was hard. He was very upset about everything that was going on then. He probably died of a broken heart," she explained. *Or of starvation*, I thought, from not being able to chew.

Going from Poland to Belgium was not complicated in 1931. There was no question of having papers, passports, visas, or immigration documents for Jews leaving the shtetls in those days. One hired a "professional" smuggler who took you to wherever you wanted to go. For a certain sum of money, he would make all the arrangements for traveling (by train), food, lodgings (open fields, farmhouses, stables), and checkpoint crossings. In each country there were places where there were no guards at the borders, especially at night, or where the guards could be bribed to let people pass. The smugglers were paid to know their way around.

"Of course, once you got to that country," my mother explained, "you had no status whatsoever, no papers—which meant that you couldn't work legally. But the Polish Jews from shtetls never did work legally, and wherever there were Jews, you got work all the same.

"My grandmother paid for the smuggler for me; one-half now, one-half when I would reach Antwerp. The smuggler was well known in Skierniewice and knew my family. There was no way he could cheat me and get away with it; too many people to answer to."

My mother, three other women, who were sisters, and the smuggler left Poland in the spring of 1931. They rode trains, then got off before the borders, suitcases in hand, and walked several miles before reaching Germany. They had been told to take as little as possible since they would have to carry it on long hikes. After a while Golda began to feel as though her arms were going to fall off, although she had brought very little and had thought her suitcase as light as a feather at the beginning of the journey. Of the landscape, she remembered very little, because they mostly traveled at night when it was safer. The smuggler had made the journey many times: he knew which house would agree to shelter and feed them, although the sleeping accommodations were very primitive. They usually spent the night in someone's stable or shared one room, which usually meant that someone wound up on the floor with a blanket, if she was lucky. Many times they slept outdoors under some trees while they waited for a safe time to cross, when the guards or policemen would be gone from the edge of the towns or the borders. Their food was mostly bread.

In spite of the smuggler's experience, the four women were always worried. What if they were caught and arrested? Would they be put in prison? "The worst thing that could happen is that you would be sent back to Poland, to Skierniewice. They won't put you in prison," the smuggler reassured them. "If you're illegal, they don't want you in their country, so they won't keep you in their jails." Nevertheless, having to be on the alert constantly, to be careful, quiet, quick, was nerve-racking. And all that walking was hard. Golda began to regret leaving Skierniewice. Maybe it had been a mistake?

From Germany, they crossed into Belgium, first stopping in Brussels, the final destination of the other three women.

"I remember that first night in Brussels," my mother told me. "The place we stopped at was a barbershop. The three women's sister and her husband had an apartment above the shop, on the second floor. It was too late for me to go on to Antwerp, so I spent the night with them. The smuggler had friends in Brussels, and he went off, promising to be back for me in the morning. I guess he thought those people would take care of me that night. Well, they didn't. They left me in the shop and told me I could sleep in one of the barber chairs and use a towel as a blanket. They went upstairs and had a big dinner to celebrate the arrival of the sisters from Poland. But they didn't invite me; they didn't give me anything to eat or drink, and I was starving. I even had to find the bathroom on my own, which was an outhouse in the courtyard. It was dark and cold outside. I think that it was the hardest night of the whole trip for me. Their rejection and indifference really hurt me, and I was scared that all the Jews in Belgium were going to be like that. But then I thought of my brother, and I knew that he would be glad to see me."

The next day the smuggler came back to fetch my mother. They took the train to Antwerp, then a bus to Fischel's house. "Door-to-door service," said the smuggler. He had picked Golda up at her grandparents' house in Skierniewice, Poland, and brought her right to Fischel's doorstep in Antwerp, Belgium. Fischel probably signed a receipt so that Golda's grandmother would part with the rest of the money owed to the smuggler.

Brother and sister were very glad to see each other. Golda was relieved that the journey was over and that she had finally arrived. From then on, she never regretted leaving Poland. She missed her older sister, Henna, and her father, but as hard as it was for her in

Antwerp when she would quarrel with her sister-in-law, when she had trouble finding work or people laughed at her Polish accent or was afraid they would guess she wore a wig, she remembered what life had been like for her in Jeżów and Skierniewice and was glad that she had left.

Fischel was happy to have her around. She was the only family he had in Antwerp. He and Golda had really hoped to have their sister Henna come over too. Then the three siblings would be together. Through all the problems in Poland with their stepmother, stingy grandparents, and greedy in-laws, and through all the hardships, the sisters and brother had stuck together, helping one another, with Fischel and Henna watching over Golda.

Henna never did come. First her husband didn't want to leave his parents, then the baby got sick, then Henna was afraid to travel because she was pregnant again, and then it was too late. She was probably herded into the Lodz ghetto with the other Jews from Skierniewice in 1941, and from there she was sent to a concentration camp. My mother never knew what happened to her, but it isn't difficult to guess.

Fischel and my mother stopped hearing from Henna when the war broke out. Afterward, there was no trace of anyone—not of the grandmother who was stingy or the grandfather who limped, the step-siblings who were sickly or the stepmother who was probably nursing, or the aunts, uncles, and cousins. They simply vanished, as did Henna, who had loved her brother Fischel and who at the age of ten had tried to mother Golda, consoling her when the other kids made fun of her scabby and bald scalp.

ANTWERP: A WEDDING, 1938

It did not take my mother long to find work in Antwerp, which in the 1930s had a large Jewish population made up mostly of illegal refugees from various Eastern European countries. These immigrants had created a rich Jewish cultural and social life centered on the Yiddish language, which they all spoke with various accents reflecting the countries they had left. Yiddish newspapers, reviews, journals, magazines, theaters, cabaret shows, debating teams, and athletic clubs were thriving, as were restaurants that served kosher food. A certain esprit de corps reigned over this community, which helped immigrants find jobs, apartments, and friends.

At first Golda lived with Fischel and worked with him in a shoe factory that made only the top part of shoes; the soles were made elsewhere, and a third place put the shoes together. She was conscientious, scrupulously honest, and not afraid of hard work, which earned her a good reputation, but she didn't like the job. Because she was an experienced seamstress, having learned to sew in Poland, she soon left the shoe factory for a job that involved sewing. After a while, she moved out of Fischel's house and got an apartment of her own. Her brother was opposed to the move, as was Rachel, his wife. The two women were getting along better now than they had in Poland, and Rachel felt she could use some help around the house, which was one of the reasons my mother wanted to move out. She was very fond of her little niece, Leah, and her eight-year-old nephew, Abraham, but she felt that she didn't have to live there in order to see them.

Because Golda was only nineteen years old, her brother felt she was too young to be completely on her own, so he persuaded her to come over every night for supper. This way she would be sure to eat well, and Fischel and Rachel could keep an eye on her; she was expected to make a financial contribution for the food. However, the arrangement did not work out. After toiling all day sewing in a factory, my mother felt she should not have to help with dinner and cleanup. Besides, she was paying for the meals, which meant she was entitled to take it easy while Rachel prepared dinner. This did not sit well with her sister-in-law, who thought it scandalous that one woman should wait on another one, and a younger one at that. Furthermore, Golda didn't like her sister-in-law's cooking; she also didn't like being accountable for her evenings. She rather enjoyed being alone at night in her own place, where she could relax, take off her girdle, go barefoot, and sit in her underwear if she felt like doing so. Most of all, she could remove her wig and walk around with her scalp bare, which she was sure was good for it.

She hadn't quite given up on finding a cure for her baldness. If fact, although she would admit it to no one, one reason she had wanted to leave Poland and come to Belgium was that she considered Belgium a much more medically advanced country where she could probably find a doctor who would help her. She hadn't looked for one yet, but she planned to do so as soon as she saved some money.

Within a few months, my mother was integrated into the Jewish community of Antwerp; she made friends and began to have a social life. She learned Flemish, the official language of Antwerp, and after a while she spoke it without the accent that had marked her as an immigrant at first. Although she had had almost no formal education, she had a good ear for languages—a knack that saved her life during the war when she carried false papers giving her a Belgian citizenship; her authenticity was never questioned when she was asked to show identification.

In Antwerp, my mother also started having boyfriends. Mostly she went out with groups of young people, but there was often a man who sooner or later singled her out, arranged it so that he was the one to sit opposite her in cafés, walk next to her on strolls, or get off the tramway at her stop.

Men's attraction to her was not surprising. In the few photographs I saw of my mother in those days, I could tell that she was beautiful, in spite of the affliction she took such pains to conceal. She had some hair at the base of her scalp which she arranged in such a fashion that her hairdo did not give away her wig. She had high cheekbones, very large dark eyes, a straight short nose, and a rather round olive-skinned face with a flawless complexion. Witty and fun loving, she adored the movies and the theater. I picture her as a young attractive woman making her way in Antwerp, enjoying a life that wouldn't last very long. It is always difficult to imagine how your mother looked or acted before your birth, especially if no one who knew her then is still alive to tell you what she was like. I know that she had a self-deprecating, ironic sense of humor because it was still present more than a half a century later when I last visited her a few months before her death in an assisted-living home.

Mostly what I heard from her during my childhood emphasized the raw deal that life had served her, and how important it was for the two of us to stick together since no one would ever love me or care for me the way she did. It was hard to deny these observations, but many times her love felt more like a burden to me than a gift. In spite of her warnings, I did not see the world as hostile, and the solidarity she demanded from me made me feel guilty when I chafed under it.

In Antwerp in the 1930s, she was leery of the masculine attention that her looks earned her, feeling that if the men discovered her "secret," they would no longer be interested in her. Though she enjoyed male company, she kept a certain distance, a certain aloofness, from her boyfriends. It was probably this, as much as her beauty, that made her attractive to the opposite sex; she seemed so strong, so sure of herself, so unabashedly frank and able to take care of herself.

On one of her social outings, Golda met my father, Moishe Chaim Katz. She was not particularly attracted to him because he was not her physical type; she liked tall, dark, strong-looking men, and who doesn't? Moishe was short and angular, skinny; he seemed to be all bones and sharp edges. He had carrot-red hair and gray-blue eyes. He looked English or Irish—a *sheygets*, definitely non-Jewish. I look very much like him, which served me well during the war, because as a blond, blue-eyed child, I easily passed for Christian.

My father was not of Golda's Polish set. His family had come to Belgium legally with the proper visas from Czechoslovakia years before, and that gave him a certain status in my mother's eyes, but his family was also one of the problems in their relationship. There were seven sisters and brothers, the youngest merely six years old, and they were all living together in a big house on Statestrasse, in Antwerp. Moishe at twenty-four was the middle child, and to Golda, who had been on her own since she was sixteen, the fact that he still lived at home seemed a sign of weakness and immaturity.

"They need me," Moishe would say, adding that his father didn't want him to move out and he respected him too much to disobey. The old man with his black hair and full gray beard did look formidable, like an ancient prophet of the Bible. He reminded Golda of her own father in Jeżów, and she could have easily warmed to him had he let her. But she sensed from the beginning that he disliked and disapproved of her. He would ask his son what he knew of Golda's family. How did he know that they were good Jews? Why was she in Antwerp without them? And how could she have left them?

Moishe tried to explain that Golda had to leave, her mother having died when she was a child, and that her older brother, who was married and had children, took care of her. He said that her grandparents were well-known, rich people in Skierniewice; they had a very good reputation. There were lots of people here in Antwerp who could vouch for them. In truth, he had met only one man who knew the family in Poland, the smuggler, who was still plying his trade and would periodically show up in Antwerp. But Moishe would have been inclined to think highly of Golda's family had she come from the moon, for he was smitten with her and determined to marry her.

"If her grandparents are so rich, why didn't they provide for her?" persisted Moishe's father. He had many other questions and could not be persuaded that my mother came from a respectable Jewish family.

Moishe knew that the idea of marriage was hopeless for the time being, and so he did not continue the conversation with his father. The old man was shocked by my mother's lack of family connections, by her independence: a young woman simply did not leave her family to live on her own in a foreign country. He thought it showed a lack of character and respect on her part, and his wife shared his feelings. Besides, they both felt that Moishe should not be the first of their children to get married since he wasn't the oldest.

Moishe's sisters were no warmer to my mother. Ethel and Malka, who were older than Moishe, looked like him. They had angular, bony bodies, red hair, and pale complexions full of freckles. Perhaps they were jealous of my mother's dark good looks, or perhaps Golda mistook their shyness for coldness, but the three women did not become friends. The other sister, Dvoirah, who was only six, was too young to be an issue. Mannes, Moishe's older brother, was friendlier toward her, but he was rarely around and therefore not much of an ally. Berel, the youngest boy, was only eight.

But Golda did have an ally in eleven-year-old Benjamin, who was enthralled by her and who adored his older brother Moishe. Benjamin was a very bright, precocious boy and became their go-between when Moishe was forbidden by their father to see her. Decades later, when I visited Benjamin in Israel, he told me of the role he had played in their relationship, his eyes twinkling at the memory of his cleverness then. "I carried messages back and forth, brought small gifts, repeated conversations, became indispensable to their courtship," he bragged. At that time, my mother couldn't believe that Moishe, at twenty-four, let his father tell him what to do, which meant they had to see each other secretly.

If Golda wasn't impressed by my father's looks, she was very taken by his sense of humor and his cheerful disposition. My mother told me that he always seemed to be in a good mood, saw the bright side of things. People were attracted to him because he had a knack for making them feel good—a talent he apparently still had in Auschwitz, according to Arnold Golde, one of his surviving campmates: even then he was still the life of the party.

He was also thoughtful, considerate, very tender, and given to romantic exaggerations, which flattered my mother during their courtship but would exasperate her once she became his wife, when she came to feel that his spontaneity was a sign of irresponsibility. Like her, he loved movies and the theater, although he preferred music. He also liked playing with children in his neighborhood, which Golda interpreted later as his excuse to get out of work, since he would often then be distracted, forget the time, and show up late for important appointments.

He was also madly in love with her, to which she could not remain indifferent. Still, my mother was seeing other men, one in particular—another Pole, David Landau, who did not question her origins and who had a trade. He was a butcher, whereas Moishe Chaim, my father, had no profession and seemed to earn money doing a dozen different things. He had many projects that never came to fruition. He had once studied to be a cantor; he had a beautiful voice, but as he had never stuck to anything else, he did not stick to this either. Besides, he didn't like the religious life well enough to see himself as a cantor.

I don't know how eager my mother was to marry my father, but I think she felt that if he loved her as much as he said he did, he should have ignored his family's objections and set a date for the wedding; his loyalty should have been to her and not to them. For now, he begged her to be patient, telling her that his parents would change their mind about their getting married.

"We'll see," said Golda, but she didn't stop seeing Landau the butcher, who also wanted to marry her but wouldn't say when.

One day when my mother came home from work, two men who identified themselves as plainclothes police officers were waiting for her at her doorstep. They asked to see her papers.

"Papers, what papers?" asked Golda with a dark foreboding.

"Your identification card. Are you a Belgian citizen?" they asked.

"Yes, of course," she lied, and when asked to prove it, she made up an elaborate story about her citizenship papers being kept by her brother, who had to leave the country to go to a funeral. She was stalling for time but knew that she was caught.

The policemen discovered that not only was she not a citizen but she had no legal papers whatsoever: no visa, no passport, no residence permit. They were amazed that she had managed to get by so long without being detected.

"I wasn't harming anyone. Who denounced me?" she asked.

The policemen assured her that no one denounced her but that they made periodic checks in her neighborhood; then they put her in jail.

When she was telling me this story, my mother still thought that it was the concierge of her building who alerted the police. The woman had taken offense when Golda refused to tip her on New Year's Day, as was the custom in Antwerp. For my mother, the first of January was not a holiday and, besides, she felt the woman didn't do her job well when she cleaned the halls and the stairs. The concierge bore her a grudge, and from that day on left her mail downstairs and made no pretense of cleaning the stairs leading up to her apartment.

My mother had not learned that it was unwise to get on the wrong side of a concierge who had much information about everyone living in the building. All visitors had to buzz her bell to be allowed in and tell her whom they had come to see. Since she delivered the mail and packages, she could tell much about the tenants' lifestyle, especially if she went through their garbage, which Golda was convinced she did. Most of all, the concierges were very close to the police, who often used them as informants precisely because they knew so much about the people in their buildings.

"What will happen to me?" asked Golda when it was finally established that she was from Skierniewice, Poland, and that she had entered Belgium illegally.

"Nothing," the police reassured her, "you will be sent back to Poland. Don't worry—you won't be in jail long."

For my mother, going back to Poland was worse than being in jail: she knew the life that awaited her there. She could not face the oppression of the shtetl, and it would be humiliating to be controlled by her grandmother again. Here, at least, she had been independent. She had a job, an apartment, friends, boyfriends; she had a life.

As soon as Moishe heard what had happened, he came to see her in jail.

"Don't worry," he said. "I know a lawyer. I'll get you out of here. They'll never send you back to Poland, never. Not while I'm alive."

As usual, he was being melodramatic, my mother told me, but she was grateful for his presence.

"I'll get you out of here. You'll see," he assured her.

He came daily, sometimes twice a day, during the week that she was held. He brought food, some clothes, even cookies that Ethel and Malka had baked for her. The sisters seemed to like her better now that she was locked up. Not a word from Landau, the butcher.

"I couldn't come," he apologized later. "I'm also illegal." But Golda was bitter.

Soon Moishe came up with the solution. "If you marry me," he told her, "you can stay. They will put you on my residency permit."

It was true. If she married a "legal" foreigner, one who had the required visa and residency permit, she would share his status, which would allow her to remain in Belgium.

"We were going to get married, anyway," said Moishe, forgetting that my mother had never said she would. When she asked about his father's objections, he looked embarrassed.

"Well, we wouldn't be married by a rabbi, not at first," he told her.

"Just a civil ceremony, so that you can be legal. My father wouldn't have to know."

"So, if he's not to know, how will we live together, how will we be as man and wife?" she wondered.

"We won't live together at first, not until we're married by a rabbi," he answered.

"Some wedding, some marriage!" exclaimed Golda.

"It's the only solution," Moishe answered. "If you are sent to Poland, you won't be able to come back. I'll never see you again. You don't want to go."

No, she did not want to go. But how humiliating to be married on the sly like that, with nobody knowing, as though she were a criminal someone had taken pity upon. She was no criminal; she had done nothing wrong. There were many people without papers in Antwerp, Jews from all over Poland and other countries. Just her luck, she thought, that she was one of the few who were caught.

But it was the only way out. She couldn't go back. There was no one else she wanted to marry. But even though she was not very religious, the idea of not having the religious ceremony really bothered her; it really would not be a wedding otherwise.

Then she thought about her baldness. Moishe didn't know. She had to tell him, but what if he changed his mind after finding out? How humiliating! And he might tell everyone, out of spite. She could get away with not telling him; after all, they weren't going to be living together; he wouldn't have to know. For the evenings that they would be spending together, she could be as careful as she had been up to now.

But that wasn't right. What if once he found out, he felt that he had been tricked into marrying her? She couldn't bear that possibility. She was much too proud. Better to go back to Poland than to be accused of tricking a man into marriage.

From what my mother told me, my father never felt that he had been tricked. Years later, when the marriage went bad and they argued about everything, as people do when they no longer get along, and their differences rubbed each other the wrong way, he never once alluded to her baldness.

"It makes absolutely no difference to me. I love you for yourself, and not your hair. How could that possibly change my feelings? Besides, if we were religious, you'd have to shave your head and wear a wig. We'll just pretend that we're orthodox. From now on, I'll wear a yarmulke, like a religious man. You always told me that my red hair made me look like a *sheygets*. This way, I'll certainly look Jewish."

Leave it to Moishe to joke about such matters, thought Golda, *and there is a difference between wearing a wig because you want to observe Jewish laws and wearing one because you have no choice.* She kept these thoughts to herself.

Golda spent seven days in jail. She sent away for her birth certificate, which was in Polish and which her father had kept for her. In May 1935 she and Moishe Chaim Katz were married in a civil ceremony, and Golda was allowed to remain in Belgium as the wife of a legal alien.

After the ceremony, Golda resumed the life of an unmarried woman. She worked, lived, and ate alone most of the time. If Moishe spent the evening and part of the night with her, he would always leave afterward to go home. My mother felt her life had changed. She did not keep up with her friends. She was angry that none of them had come to see her in jail. No one had offered to help, although it wasn't clear what they could have done; she knew that most of them were as illegal as she was and had been afraid to be asked for papers at the police station—but still, she had felt deserted and abandoned. Besides, now that she was married, she could not be as carefree and fun loving as before. She could not keep on flirting with men, and most of the relationships she had had with men were of a flirtatious nature. She had become quite skillful at arousing their interest but keeping them at arm's length when their interest turned sexual. In part her fear of being "discovered" and therefore spurned had made her lead a chaste life before marrying my father.

She began to pressure my father into "really" marrying her and assuming his role as her husband.

"Neither here nor there. I'm not really married, and I'm not really free. What kind of a life is that with you going home every night to your family? If you love them that much, why did you marry me? Just to do me a favor?" she asked, forgetting that he had done so for her to be able to stay in Belgium.

Moishe, of course, denied it and asked her to be patient.

Fischel, Golda's brother, was furious when he found out. "What kind of nonsense is that?" he asked when Golda told him about her marriage and wept on his shoulder.

"That comes from being so independent and always wanting to be on your own," said Rachel, who then asked her if she was pregnant.

"No, of course not," Golda answered, rather offended. But Rachel was not convinced, and from that time on started watching my mother's belly.

Three years later, in 1938, Ethel's beau finally declared himself, and the oldest child of the Katz clan was married. Then Mannes, Moishe's older brother, got engaged. Nothing happened with Malka, whose name meant "queen," but Moishe decided that it was all right not to wait for the queen to be spoken for and told his father that he wanted to marry Golda. His father did not object by then, having foreseen that eventuality. Although he had never said anything, the old man knew about their clandestine encounters. My little uncle Benjamin wasn't as clever as he had thought.

In June of that year, Moishe, then twenty-eight years old, and Golda, who was twenty-five, were married by a rabbi, under a canopy, a chuppah, with full religious fanfare. Golda wore a white satin dress and held a bouquet of calla lilies in her hands; she looked smashing. Moishe wore a top hat slightly tilted on his long head, and a white carnation in his lapel; he looked rather dapper in a Fred Astaire sort of way. (I still have that photograph, one of the only three that I have of my mother and father together.)

The immediate family posed for a group portrait. The young married couple sat in the middle; the father of the groom, my *zeyde*, looking surprisingly happy, sat on Moishe's side, his wife, wearing the religious black wig, sat next to Golda, then all the Katz siblings stood around them: Ethel and her husband, Malka, Mannes and his intended, twelve-year-old Berel, ten-year-old Dvoirah, and Benjamin looking smug as though he had been the one to pull off the ceremony. Also in the photograph are Fischel and his wife, Rachel—who was certain this time that Golda had to be pregnant—their daughter, Leah, who at seventeen had begun to turns heads and was always chosen to play the beautiful Queen Esther in Purim festivals, and their son, Abraham.

My mother's side was also represented by the Wunderman family, who had left Poland decades before. There was Henna Wunderman, Golda's father cousin who had the same name as Golda's older sister, and who like her sister had done her best to serve as Golda's surrogate parent. Henna was a resourceful person who had been most helpful to Golda when she first arrived in Antwerp, finding her an apartment and work when Golda left the shoe factory. She continued to be helpful whenever Golda turned to her, until her death five years after the war.

Standing on a chair in the back was Henna's charming but unemployable husband, Nathan; the Wunderman children, fourteen-year-old Bella and five-year-old Max, were sitting on the floor in the front of everyone. Twenty people posing together for the last time. They did not know then there would be no more gatherings: no more weddings, no more bar mitzvahs, not even any more funerals since Jewish funerals would be forbidden by German law, two years later, when Belgium was occupied. When Moishe's father died in 1942, he was buried with no accompanying Jewish ceremony.

Twenty people in the photograph; sixteen would be dead in six years: Auschwitz, Buchenwald, Dachau . . . Pretty Leah was never heard from again after she reported as instructed to the deportation bureau on avenue Louise in Brussels. Fischel, suspicious Rachel, who for once was not suspicious enough, and their son, Abraham, were deported from Brussels and gassed as soon as they stepped off the train in Poland.

My father's mother; his older brother Mannes and Mannes's wife;

his sister Ethel and her reluctant husband and their two-year-old son, Joseph; his sister Malka the queen, sixteen-year-old brother Berel, and fourteen-year-old sister Dvoirah—all of them disappeared after they were arrested. Moishe's father died of "natural causes."

"He died of a broken heart, from knowing what was happening to everyone," said my uncle Benjamin, decades later in Israel. Clever and resourceful Benjamin had been sent to Auschwitz at seventeen and survived, proving that perhaps he was as resourceful and clever as he had claimed to be in Antwerp, but probably because he was simply lucky.

The dapper bridegroom, Moishe, my father, was sent to various concentration camps in 1942 and wound up in Auschwitz in 1944.

The Wunderman family miraculously survived the war intact: Bella was hidden in a convent, Max in an asylum for tuberculosis patients, and Simon—the youngest, born in 1938, after Golda and Moishe's wedding—as the only little boy with sight in a home for blind children. The parents, Henna and Nathan, managed to remain in Brussels with counterfeit papers.

My mother also survived, living in Brussels, taking the identity of a Belgian gentile woman by the name of Jeanne Van Hollander; she had papers this time, but they were forged. As for me, Moishe and Golda's daughter, born one year after their wedding and one year before the Germans invaded Belgium, I survived by being hidden with a Catholic family in Beersel, a small village south of Brussels that I now wanted to find again.

Manneken-Pis—the statue of a chubby, naked little boy with a mischievous smile and a tiny penis urinating in a fountain basin—is a trademark of Brussels, and one of the most visited tourist sites in the city. There are several stories that explain the origin of the statue, but I prefer the one that claims it was erected by grateful parents who were looking for their lost child and finally found him peeing in the street. The lost child I was looking for when I got to this city was myself at the age of three, and the parents I wanted to find were those of the family who took me in and hid me after my father's arrest and deportation.

I had a place to stay in Brussels because Myriam and Esther, my new filmmaking friends who were back in New York, had given me the key to an apartment they used in the city. They told me to use the telephone; the refrigerator was full of food. This was my first time back to Belgium since I had left it in 1952 for the United States. I couldn't help comparing my arrival here now with that of my mother about fifty years before. Whereas she had been paperless, lacking visas, passports, and money, I came with my American passport and a credit card in good standing. She had come to build a future; I was coming to rescue a past. But she had arrived to be part of a family and of a large welcoming Jewish community; I was here alone, my family not erased by old age but snatched by the war against the Jews.

Myriam and Esther had given me the name of friends, a couple who would help me in my search. Richard and his wife were born in Belgium in the mid- and late 1940s. Their parents had to hide during the war; they had lost relatives. Like any Jews in Europe, they had been affected. When I called them, they invited me to dinner. That evening I told them that I wanted to find the people who had hidden me forty years ago and for whom I had an address in Beersel, and that I also wanted to find the orphanage where I had spent time after the war ended. I had no address for that institution, but I knew it had been in the small village of La Hulpe within driving distance of Brussels. How many orphanages could a village have? Richard offered to drive me to both places and to help me find what I was looking for.

I accepted his offer with gratitude. And so Richard became my "chauffeur," driving me from Brussels to Beersel to La Hulpe, back to Brussels and to Beersel again. I had hoped to stay in touch with him, but shortly after I returned to America, he and his wife divorced, both moved, and I lost track of him.

I could hardly sleep that night thinking about the possibility of finding the Walschots. Could they still be alive? How would they react to seeing me? Would they remember me? Were they angry with me for never contacting them, for not writing, for never thanking them enough? Would I like them? Would they like me? What sort of people were they? How awkward would it be?

The next morning, Sunday, Richard showed up punctually at eight o'clock to drive me to Beersel in a beautiful black Lincoln sedan. I had remembered the Beersel of my childhood as worlds away from Brussels, yet we reached it in less than an hour. As we drove into the city, my heart sank: Those bright little villas with their careful lawns were obviously new; the smart apartment buildings looked so modern—would there be anything left of the old Beersel? The streets were empty, and all the shops were closed. We had trouble finding people to ask for directions as we looked for chaussée d'Uccle, the address I had for the Walschots. Finally, as we were driving very slowly toward the older center part of town, we went by a block of stone houses. My heart started racing. "Stop," I yelled, and jumped out of the car without being conscious of why I was doing it. I ran up to the first red old house. "This is it," I yelled. "I know this is it." Something about the building stirred an excitement in me. I felt a great joy and comfort even before I saw the number: 170. We were on chaussée d'Uccle right in front of the Walschot house. I had somehow recognized it. There was a piece of paper under the doorbell with a handwritten name "Walschot." I couldn't believe it; after forty years, they were still living here, in the same house. It was so easy—a forty-minute ride from Brussels, and I had caught up with my past. I rang and rang the doorbell. No answer. Only then did I admit what I had refused to acknowledge when I first spotted the house: It was all boarded up; the iron shutters of each window were closed, as were those of the house next door and the one next to it.

After coming all this way, I didn't want to give up now, so I decided to try the other houses on the street. I rang the doorbell next door; no answer. I tried the next house, the next, and the next, in spite of them also being boarded up. No answer anywhere. The street was empty. No cars came by.

As I kept on moving down the quiet street, I heard a radio from a building; its garage door was ajar. I pushed on the door and it opened. After crossing through the garage, I found myself in a vegetable garden. The garage had an L-shaped extension; a sort of small apartment was attached to it, and lively accordion music was coming from inside. I knocked. No answer, but the radio was turned off. I knocked again, this time much louder and longer. After a while the curtain of window in the door was drawn. The face of an old man appeared, suspicious.

"Monsieur," I said in French, "I want to ask you some information, please help me."

"What do you want?" he asked.

"I want to know about number 170. Who lives there?"

"The Walschots," he replied.

"The Walschot family that lived there during the war?" I asked.

"Yes," he said. A little less cautious now, he opened the door slightly. He added, "Who else?"

I asked him if he knew where they were.

"I don't know," he replied. "On vacation like everyone else; in Portugal or Italy—who knows? I didn't ask, they didn't tell me."

"Aren't they a little old to travel?" I asked.

"Old?" he replied, "Marguerite and her children aren't old."

"Who is Marguerite?" I asked.

"Marguerite Walschot is who lives there," he replied.

"But I thought you meant Franz Walschot and his wife. That's who I'm looking for."

"Oh, them! They're dead."

It didn't sink in at first: So many contradictory bits of information to digest and feelings to go through. First the excitement of thinking that I found the Walschots, then learning that it wasn't them. "Who is Marguerite?" I asked again. He told me that she was the Walschots' granddaughter who had gotten divorced and had reclaimed her maiden name. She lived in the house with her children.

He looked at me puzzled, wondering why I was asking all these questions. His answers had been somewhat reluctant at first, but now he opened his door and stepped out of his apartment. He wanted to know what this was all about: Richard, so dapper in his camel-hair coat; the fancy car parked outside; my persistence. He spoke French with a Flemish accent. Beersel is a Flemish-speaking village, but since I no longer spoke the language, I continued in French. I decided to tell him the truth—that I was asking all those questions because as a child I had lived with the Walschots during the war.

"Oh, you're the little Jewish girl they were hiding," he exclaimed, smiling.

Richard and I looked at each other in great surprise. "I remember you," he went on, "in fact, I thought you looked familiar."

I was too stunned to say anything. All these years, I had thought it was a big secret, had assumed my life depended on that secrecy, and here was a neighbor who had known the big secret all along! Richard asked how he felt about the Walschots hiding a Jewish child.

"It was none of my business," he replied. "Besides," he added, "the whole village knew. We weren't *Boches*, you know. Why should we care?" (*Boches* is a pejorative French term for Germans.)

He affected casual indifference, but he was looking at me intensively.

"What happened to the Walschots?" I asked.

"The old ones? She died about twenty years ago, of cancer." When I asked what had been her first name, he replied: "Régine, of course."

Now it made sense. Régine had been too hard for me to pronounce at three, so I had called her Gine, Mama Gine.

He told me that Franz, her husband, went to live with a daughter after that. He had died two or three years ago.

I had missed him by just a few years. If only I had looked for them sooner, if only I had known it would be so easy to find them. Now I would never see them again. I just couldn't believe it; to find them only to lose them. When I asked how he died, he told me that Franz Walschot died of old age. I had been right in remembering them as older, even though they had a fourteen-year-old daughter, Jeanne, who had been like a sister to me. They must have been in their fifties when I lived with them.

"He was in his nineties, like me, when he died," the old man said, then added proudly, "but I never felt better in my life."

Monsieur Waltins, as he gave his name, did look very sturdy. Slightly heavy with rosy cheeks and thick white hair, he was the picture of health. By now, he had become very friendly and talkative. "Where do you live now?" he asked.

"America."

"Ah, America. Land of opportunity! You can see the Walschot garden from here," he went on. "I bought up all the houses on the block."

"You mean their garden is behind this house?" I asked.

"Yes," he answered, "just walk to this wall for a view."

The wall he mentioned was only a few feet high; I straddled it easily. He started to say something, then shrugged his shoulders. I was in the Walschot garden, which had been a magical place for me as a child, but it bore only a distant resemblance to my memory of it. There was a chicken coop now in disuse, a rabbit hutch, an old collapsed building that used to be the outhouse, and an orchard; everything was there. I especially remembered the orchard with its flowering apple, pear, and cherry trees. My job had been to sit under them, alone, and bang on the lid of a pot to make enough noise to scare the blackbirds away from the fruit. I was always afraid that while I was sitting there, everyone in the house would pack up and leave.

An apartment building stood where I had remembered an expanse of green.

"Wasn't there a field there?" I asked M. Waltins.

"Yes," he answered. "Sold it, and for a pretty penny, I might say."

I remembered the sheep in those fields. Another one of my jobs had been to watch them. One of them had ran away one day, and I cried and cried, because I couldn't bear the idea of the sheep not finding its way back and wandering all alone. I was sure that it was my fault. Now the Walschots would no longer love me; now they would turn me over to the bad Germans. I did not know exactly what this meant, but I had been led to believe that this was the worst thing that could happen; that much had been drilled into my head.

I hadn't gone home that day, afraid to be punished for the loss of the sheep. I hid when they came looking and calling for me. Eventually they found me. The spanking I got was not for losing the sheep, which they found the next day, but for worrying them.

As I now walked in the neglected garden, I was filled with a great joy, and I realized that I had been happy here living with the Walschots for a year and a half. I had images of sitting on Papa Franz's lap, of drawing and coloring pictures next to Jeanne, Mama Gine at the stove, warming up some milk for me. A quiet family life had usurped memories of my mother and the still-vaguer remembrances of my red-haired father.

"You know, there is a son who lives in town," said M. Waltins. I hadn't remembered a son, only a girl, Jeanne, about fourteen. "They had two other children, much older, who were already married during the war. The son is Martin; the woman was Rosa—her daughter Marguerite is the one who lives at this address now," he added. He didn't know where Jeanne was, but he thought Martin might know. Martin lived on a street that was easy to find, right behind the church on the main square. "A house with a red door, lots of flowers," Waltins said. "Just ask anybody; they'll know." His description turned out to fit almost all the houses in the village.

We chatted some more. I kept asking him questions, checking out my memories. Yes, there used to be a café/restaurant across the street; closed down twenty years ago. Yes, of course, the village had been occupied. He told me that the Germans had been stationed in the Hotel de Ville, the town hall, in the center of town, a few blocks away from the house.

It struck me as ironic that I was "hiding" so close to the Germans, but then I wasn't supposed to be Jewish, or at least had assumed that no one knew I was.

"Did the Germans ever come down this street?" I asked.

"Sometimes, not often. They came to the café, but there was a bigger, better restaurant on the main square. It's still there. The Germans would go there," he replied.

I remember their visit once to our house. I was taken up to the attic and told to stay there until Jeanne came and fetched me again. I don't think I was very scared then; it had seemed more of a game.

M. Waltins let Richard take a picture of the two of us together in front of number 170. In the photograph, he came out clearly looking like a strong, old man with his white visor cap, his ruddy cheeks, and his belly bulging slightly in his green American polo shirt. My face, with its worried look, on the other hand, is barely visible under the effusive, black curls of my bohemian hairdo; my pink and purple long skirt was a splash of brilliant color against the white door of the Walschot home.

"If you want to know more, I'm usually home; come back and visit," he said as we were leaving.

It struck me that he was perhaps a little lonely, all by himself on a fine Sunday in July, with all the neighbors gone on vacation. We thanked him and went off looking for Martin Walschot.

Martin wasn't as easy to find as M. Waltins had claimed. The streets around the main square did not conform to the old man's description. The few people walking by knew of no Martin Walschot. I suppose I had fallen for the image of the small town where everyone knows everyone else because they have lived there forever. But people walking by were friendly, eager to help. One woman in shorts, with a big shopping bag, thought she knew of a Walschot living a few streets down, a guard or a policeman.

No, she didn't know the name of the street, but you couldn't miss the house; it stood by itself on a corner, had a little garden, a white picket fence, lots of flowers. It sounded like the one M. Waltins had described. After asking directions a few more times from other people, we found the house. It was freshly painted in bright colors and surrounded by rows of flowers. No name on the doorbell. I rang. A child opened the door, a little girl who looked about nine years old. I asked if her father was home. No, he wasn't. Was he a policeman? Yes, he was. I thought, *Home free.* Her mother came down the stairs in a bathrobe, her hair in curlers. I explained what I wanted, how I was looking for survivors of the family who had hidden me during the war. This time, I jumped right into my story. Richard stayed discreetly in the background.

"But my husband didn't grow up here," said the woman. "He wasn't here during the war." It turned out that his parents were not Franz and Régine, and that he himself was from Charleroi. Wrong Walschots. "I'm sorry," continued the woman. "I'd let you speak to him, but he's not here; he went fishing. Would you like a cup of coffee?"

We turned down her offer and left. I felt disappointed. Finding the house, then running into M. Waltins and having him remember—all that had been so encouraging, but now we seemed to have come to a dead end. Richard was not so easily defeated. He suggested we go to the restaurant that was open on the town square and look up Martin Walschot in their telephone directory. So we went to the restaurant and chatted with the pleasant-looking waitress who brought us two cups of coffee. Yes, this restaurant was here during the war but, of course, not with the same owners. This then was the fancy restaurant the Germans had frequented. There were now many waiters and waitresses setting up tables: white tablecloth, crystal glasses, roses. There were no diners.

"Oh, it's too early yet," the waitress explained, guessing our question by our puzzled look around. "Everyone comes after church or after a walk, around one o'clock or so." Had it been that popular with the locals when it was filled with German soldiers?

We got the telephone directory and found three Walschots listed in it. One was at 170 chaussée d'Uccle, Marguerite, the granddaughter. The second was Germain, the absent policeman whose wife we had just left. The third one was a Martin Walschot, 25 Stoofstraat. No answer when we called.

"Perhaps they're in church," Richard offered. "We'll try again later."

As Richard spoke, I noticed the old Gothic church across the street; I remembered that we went there every Sunday. I told Richard I wanted to visit it.

We paid for the coffee, crossed the square, and entered the church. Mass was going on. The music and the smell of flowers and candles burning brought back images of Mama and Papa Walschot and Jeanne kneeling there, rising, sitting, and kneeling again. I remember my fascination with the statues and the stained-glass windows, and how after a while, feeling bored, I would fidget. Jeanne, who was well behaved, sat next to me, and I sometimes tried to tickle her exposed knees to make her laugh—it always worked.

I suppose all Catholic churches smell the same, share the same rituals, but for a Jewish child, it had been an enchanting place. I liked going, perhaps because it was followed by a big, special meal with treats. I liked seeing the crowd and Mama Gine all dressed up with her fancy hat.

Now I enjoyed seeing the church again. With so many changes in Beersel, it was comforting to find that some things remained the same; it gave me a sense of continuity, or at least it made those vague memories more concrete for the time being. But the feeling did not last, and after a while I no longer felt at home here. Suddenly the church seemed to lose its appeal and looked like all the other churches I had since visited in Europe as a tourist. Had it always been this small? I had remembered it as a cathedral. And the stained-glass windows showing the Madonna and child seemed generic and now no longer reminded me of my mother and me.

Leaving the church, we decided to drive to 25 Stoofstraat rather than call Martin Walschot again. The address took us out of town on a very suburban-looking road with new, pretty, well-tended little gardens. There were geranium pots on most of the house windows. Number 25 had a shiny red door with *Walschot* written in pretty script under the doorbell. No one answered when we rang; there was no one in the garden, but the house was not boarded up. Lace curtains peeped out of a second-story window that had been left open. It didn't look as if the inhabitants had gone away.

I didn't want to leave a note as Richard suggested. "No, I'd rather not. What if it's not whom I'm looking for? I have the address and phone number. I'll call tomorrow from Brussels," I told him. I think all those changes—the pretty houses with flowering gardens, the ease of reaching this village from Brussels, the spick-and-span landscapes so unlike my memories—made me feel that it was Beersel's way of erasing the war, as though those terrible years had never happened. Where did that leave me? Had I imagined my anxious childhood?

Suddenly, I felt emotionally drained and did not want to keep looking for people. Too much seemed to be hanging on luck, on coincidences. And I also felt vague stirrings of a pain I had been repressing all morning, the pain of laying claim to feelings I didn't have. Everything seemed so ordinary, so calm, so picturesque here, that I felt like an intruder in this pretty little Belgian village. Could all the fear, anxiety, and panic underneath have been something I made up? Perhaps my mother had been right and I was stirring ashes of a fire that had never burned me. I had enough of Beersel for the moment. I wanted to leave this bright, sunny cheerfulness that challenged my war memories. But I still needed to go to La Hulpe, to find the children's home where I spent a couple of years after the war. So we left Beersel.

Sitting in a café in Brussels, after returning from La Hulpe, where we had found the site of the orphanage that had been my home in 1945 and 1946, Richard talked me into telephoning Martin Walschot again. This time he was home. It was a difficult and joyful conversation; he just couldn't believe that it was little Astrid calling after forty years. He was so happy to hear from me that he begged me to come see him right away. Inundated by many contradictory feelings, I wanted to put it off, but Martin was insistent, so we drove back to Beersel.

Both Martin Walschot and I were overwhelmed by this reunion. His wife was beaming and went down the basement to fetch a bottle of wine they had saved for a special occasion. I didn't really remember him, but he talked about his parents, who had been my Papa Franz and Mama Gine, and about his little sister Jeanne, who had been my big sister.

How happy they all would have been to see me again, to know that I had been all right after I left them, he told me. How they had missed me! "My father especially always talked about you, wondering why he never heard from you," Martin said. "You two were very thick; every time I turned around, you were sitting on his lap while he taught you songs," he continued. "For a while, he would wonder every day if you were safe, as the war was still going on." Why hadn't I come earlier, he asked. Why, indeed? After the war, I had missed my father very much, not realizing that perhaps the father I yearned for was the one I really had known, Papa Franz, not Moishe Katz—who I probably didn't remember. And all this time, I had never thought about those years from the Walschots' perspective; it had never occurred to me that they might have missed me after I left. I suddenly felt the joy of having been loved as a child by that family at the same time that I felt guilt at not having tried to find them. I had been ungrateful toward a family that had run such risks in hiding me during the war. Had I, in some ways, doubted their attachment or courage? Had I been influenced all these years by my mother's attitude? Martin could not tell me why his parents had decided to defy the Germans, especially since his father had never been politically active. Perhaps by hiding me, he felt like he was resisting the occupation?

Now I would never know what their motives had been, but given their love for me, I know that kindness had played a role. But Jeanne was very much alive, and I could go to see her. Martin gave me her address; she was a grandmother now and lived with her family in Waterloo, but they were all away, like everyone else on vacation for the month. Since I couldn't spend a month in Belgium to wait for her return, I said I would write her as soon as I got back to the States.

Martin also talked about my mother that afternoon. He remembered her visits and our clandestine meetings in his tool shed. How pretty my mother had been, he told me. I had to remember that she was only around thirty years old when all this was happening. Smartly dressed but very reserved, she hardly spoke to him, he said. My mother told me, years later, that on one of her visits, he had made a pass at her that threw her into a panic. Would he take her refusal out on me? Would he denounce me to get even? It was hard to give credence to her fears looking at him now, so jovial, so happy to see me.

Richard and I didn't speak much on the way back to Brussels again; I wasn't sure what I was feeling anymore.

ANTWERP: A MARRIAGE, 1938

While my parents' wedding was a success, the marriage was not. Golda had expected my father to become a different man once he became her husband, but he didn't change his ways. Their biggest bone of contention was his relationship with his family, to whom he seemed inordinately attached. He was still very much the most responsible offspring: Ethel, whose bossy ways had dominated the household, was uninvolved because she had gotten married herself. Mannes had been completely taken over by his intended and her family. Malka, the queen, was in love and was hardly around the house. The other siblings were too young to fill Moishe's shoes.

So Moishe continued to be the dutiful son who ran errands, filled out all the paperwork that was needed, did the books for his father's faltering diamond business, and repaired things around the house, to the detriment, my mother felt, of his own home—not that he was very good at fixing things, but that was not the point. She felt he always found time for his father and family but not for his wife.

Fischel, her brother, had helped Golda and Moishe set up a shoe store, called Maison Finor, at number 1, Kortestooper Strasse. Fischel knew the business well and had connections with wholesalers who would sell on credit. The shop was on the ground floor, and there was an apartment with three large rooms on the second floor, which became my parents' home. It seemed to my mother that whenever the bell sounded, meaning someone had walked in the door, my father was not around; she was the one who had to run down the flight of stairs to wait on customers.

Soon a division of labor was established: My father would do the buying and distribution for the store, visiting showrooms and factories, filling orders, and taking the train or bus to remote places to deliver merchandise; my mother would wait in the little room behind the shop downstairs and take care of customers as they came in the store. This meant she wouldn't have to run up and down the stairs all day, which made her too tired, especially now that she was pregnant.

At first, she didn't tell my father. This was not a good time to have a baby: business was bad. Golda wasn't sure they would be able to keep the store going. There were rumors about Jews being mistreated in Poland and in Germany. Hitler was gaining strength. Czechoslovakia, my father's homeland, was occupied by the Germans. There had been outbreaks of anti-Semitic incidents in Antwerp recently. Golda did not want to bring a child into this unstable world.

She went to consult her cousin and best friend, Henna Wunderman, who had always been resourceful and helpful in many different ways. "Take lots of baths with vinegar and cold water," the woman told her. Golda gritted her teeth as she sank into the tub of ice-cold water. Nothing happened.

Henna then suggested that she try something more drastic. "The knitting needle is foolproof. I know women who tried it, and it worked. I'll help you, Golda. We'll do it here in my house so that I can take care of you," she told her.

So the next day, my mother laid on Henna's worktable, the one her husband Nathan, the tailor, used to cut cloth for her. No one was home but the two women. Golda guided the long knitting needle into her vagina. Clenching her teeth, she gave it a shove. Fear made her scream before she even felt the pain. She felt dizzy and nauseous with a great weariness at the same time. She quickly withdrew the needle; it was covered with blood.

"There, it's all over," said Henna. "You'll see; your period will come in a day or two. Everything will be all right now." Golda went home depressed, tired. By the time she got home, she was no longer bleeding. Her period did not come within a week; she was still pregnant.

"One more thing,' said Henna. "There are shots you can take that give you contractions and you lose the baby." She had a friend whose husband was a pharmacist and would give her the medication and the needle. My mother was reluctant at first, afraid the shots would be painful or dangerous, but she was assured that there was nothing to worry about; they would produce severe menstrual-like cramps that would eject the fetus. She decided to try it.

So, Cousin Henna got the vials from her pharmacist friend. He taught her how to give shots. There wasn't really much to it; you had to have the courage to pierce the skin with the needle. Henna practiced giving shots all afternoon by sticking an orange. My mother stopped by twice a day for her series of shots. After five days, she had such severe cramps that she couldn't get out of bed.

Then suddenly the cramps stopped, but the blood did not come that evening as it was supposed to nor on the next day: she was still pregnant. She was frightened by now, thinking that if I was so hard to get rid of, perhaps I was meant to be. So she stopped trying to abort and told my father that she was expecting. He was so delighted that she was convinced that had he known earlier, he would have objected to her attempts to terminate the pregnancy.

I was surprised that my mother told me the story of her attempts at aborting me, but somehow I understood and didn't blame her; my reproach was that I could have been crippled in the process. Yet that very evening, I dreamed that my mother tried to stick a needle in my eye while I slept. Perhaps I was less forgiving than I thought, but knowing what was to follow, how could I be angry at her?

In spite of her panic, my mother told me that the thought of being pregnant also filled her with moments of joy. She would catch sight of herself in a shop window and think, "I'm carrying a baby—how wonderful!" She felt somehow that she had passed a test proving that she was "normal." She had never assumed that her lack of hair would prevent her from having children; nevertheless, it was good to know that for sure, to have proof that she was like other women. (In 1941 when she became pregnant again, she found a doctor who gave her an abortion.)

Moishe and Golda settled on a name: Isaac if it was a boy; Dvoirah Aurelia if it was a girl. Golda had wanted a girl named after her mother, but her mother had been so young when she died of typhus in Poland, that superstitious as she was, Golda did not want to bring bad luck to her own daughter. Moishe's mother, Dvoirah, had died at thirty, and he wanted to name his daughter after her, even though his father had remarried and already named his daughter from that marriage Dvoirah. Thirty was not considered young enough then to be tragic or bad luck. The maternal grandmother's name would be a middle name.

They had a baby girl, me, in July 1939. Moishe went to city hall to record my birth.

"You want to call her what?" asked an incredulous clerk, not recognizing the name.

"Dvoirah," Moishe answered.

The clerk refused to register the name and told my father that he had to choose a Christian one.

My father couldn't think of a suitable name. His eyes fell on a poster hanging on the wall behind the clerk's counter. It was of the queen of Belgium, the great favorite from Sweden; he chose that name. That's the story he told my mother, but I find it still hard to believe since that very popular queen had died at a young age in a car accident, which would have been precisely the bad luck my parents had wanted to avoid in naming me. Perhaps my father wasn't aware of the queen's early death, only of her popularity.

"What kind of a name is Astrid?" asked Golda later in the hospital. They argued about it for a while, but since Moishe had had no choice and my birth registration couldn't be changed, my mother stopped her objections. They agreed that although I was legally named Astrid, at home they would always call me Dvoirah, Dorele, or Dori. So it was my father who first gave me a Christian twin who was to save my life during the war but who clung to me afterward until I turned eighteen and became a naturalized American citizen, formally changing my first name to Dori. Until then, there had been no legal documents for "Dori": no alien registration card, no passport, no school diploma, no driver's license; officially she had never existed.

In May 1940, two months before I turned one, the Belgian army, after having fought the Germans for eighteen days, surrendered at the instigation of its king, Leopold III, who asked for an armistice, which was granted and signed on May 28. Germany began its four-year occupation of Belgium. Panic broke out among the population, especially among the Jews. Moishe and Golda, like many other people, tried to escape to France. Fischel had bought a car but didn't yet know how to drive. My father could drive, so he piled Fischel, his wife, Rachel, their two children, Leah and Abraham, my mother, and me into the car and drove south. We joined the hundreds of Belgian refugees trying to flee the onslaught of the Germans by going to France, where we thought we would escape the war. Moishe's family was to follow by train. We were all supposed to meet in Lille, France, because Moishe knew someone there who would find us lodging—farmers who rented out their extra rooms and sold milk and bread to boarders.

In Lille, everyone waited five days for Moishe's family. They did not come. Moishe was very worried, but the news was reassuring. The Germans did not seem to treat Jews any differently from others in Belgium. There was a lot of registration and filling out of papers going on, but nothing else seemed to be happening. German officials made announcements on the radio telling Jews not to worry, they would not be mistreated, and that the war was over. Jews were encouraged to return home.

Moishe and Fischel drove back to Belgium to look for Moishe's family. They were all supposed to come back in a few days. They didn't. Now my mother was worried.

"What could have happened to them?" she kept asking her sister-in-law Rachel.

"I don't know," Fischel's wife answered, and added that they should go back to Belgium.

The French farmers we were staying with were less and less hospitable; they hadn't counted on having to feed and house four extra people and a baby for so long. They kept asking for more money. When almost three weeks had elapsed, Golda and Rachel decided to go back to Belgium.

So, with the farmers carrying their bags to the station, Golda, Rachel, her children, and I took the train back to Antwerp. Everyone was home. Fischel's car had broken down, and it had taken Moishe a while to find a garage willing to fix it. When the family was finally gathered and set out again, they had been turned back by the Germans as they attempted to cross the border into France. Moishe's father was not feeling well; he had wanted to go back, anyway.

At first, life went on as usual, although it seemed to my mother that wherever she turned, there were German uniforms; they were at the post office, at city hall, at the telephone counters, in parks, in movie theaters, on tramways, near newspaper kiosks, in all the stores, and especially in the streets. Moishe and Golda tried to ignore them and tend to their shoe store. One of their best customers was a German officer. The store was not in a Jewish neighborhood. Perhaps the officer didn't know the storekeepers were Jewish, seeing as he kept coming back to order boots or fancy shoes. (This was before Jewish stores were forced to put a notice in their windows declaring that they were a Jewish establishment.) During the day, I slept in a crib by the cash register. The officer always stopped by to look at me and would play with me.

"I have one just slightly older than her. What is her name?" he asked.

"Astrid," answered my mother.

"Astrid. What a beautiful name. Astrid like the queen. Astrid, Astrid," he called out.

I don't know if I answered him, but I must have flashed him a smile, because from that time on he would always bring a little milk and bread for me when he came in, or a piece of chocolate or a small toy. It made my mother nervous.

In October 1940, the first German anti-Jewish laws went into effect. No kosher butchering of meat permitted from now on, no more kosher food period. My mother said they all gave up meat and chicken, and tried to buy more fish and eggs; these quickly became more expensive.

A few days later, an ordinance giving the legal definition of a Jew was issued: three grandparents of Jewish origins, or two if they practiced their religion, made a person Jewish. Since Judaism was considered a race and not a religion, one's religious affiliation or that of one's parents did not matter; race was not a matter of choice. At home, no one needed racial laws to tell them they were Jewish.

Non-Belgian Jews who had left the country were no longer allowed to return. All Jews had to register with the AJB, the Association of Jews in Belgium agency, which was to serve as an intermediary between the Jews and the Germans. The AJB was run by the most highly reputed Jewish businessmen, philanthropists, and rabbis, who had no choice but do the Germans' bidding.

From then on, all changes in the family had to be reported and registered; any change in residence, in marital status, any birth or death—all had to be officially declared. All registers were made out in triplicate: one copy was kept by the AJB, one was sent to the Belgian authorities, and one was turned over to the Gestapo, the German police.

Only after registering as a Jew could a person go to the courthouse to receive an updated identification card. Although before the war it had been illegal in Belgium to refer to religion in official documents, now the Antwerp commune in city hall stamped a big "Jood-Juif" (Jew) on the card, and other civil authorities were told to follow suit.

My mother and father and the whole family registered with some 43,000 other Jews in Antwerp and received their "J"-marked identification cards. Fischel and his family left the city for the larger and therefore more anonymous Brussels, where no one knew them, and there they found an apartment in a non-Jewish neighborhood. Golda and Moishe didn't visit often; the car had long been confiscated by the Germans.

The next question was what to do about Maison Finor, my parents' shoe store. A new ordinance had been issued that any business or enterprise dealing with the public that was owned a quarter or more by Jews had to be registered with the AJB, again in triplicate, along with a list of assets, stock, and income generated by the business. Such businesses also had to have a large poster in the store window declaring in three languages—French, Flemish, and German—that they were Jewish establishments.

My mother was very worried about that law. "It's a way for them to take over. Once they have identified the Jewish enterprises, they'll confiscate them," she warned my father. He thought she was being too pessimistic and that the undertaking of seizing all Jewish belongings was too great a project to be possible. "You know how many people they'll have to employ to accomplish that?" he asked.

"They'll get plenty of help, you'll see," she replied.

In the long run, Moishe and Golda decided that it was best to give up the shoe store. The future looked too uncertain for them to plan to bring in stock, invest money, and accumulate debts. My mother couldn't stand the idea of that poster in the store window; it would make them so visible as Jews, so vulnerable to the anti-Semitic attacks that had been increasing in Antwerp. Her fears proved well-founded when the next ordinances made Jews declare and register all their holdings: information about all personal or business bank accounts, all stocks and bonds, all things of value from paintings to furniture and rugs to jewelry had to be revealed and recorded. Insurance companies were asked to turn over their files of Jewish customers to the German authorities, which they promptly did.

My mother and father sold their shoe store to a gentile buyer at a great loss and were told that they were lucky to find anyone willing to take the business off their hands.

Life was changing for Golda and Moishe Chaim and their families and friends. They could no longer visit each other in the evening because a Jewish curfew between 8 p.m. and 7 a.m. had been put in place. They were banned from movies, theaters, and concerts. Some restaurants and cafés had signs in their windows saying that they did not serve Jews. Eventually, my mother couldn't take me to the park anymore because it was also made off-limits.

The new ordinances affected members of the family differently depending on their circumstances. My uncle Mannes's father-in-law, whose family had lived in Belgium for over a century, was asked to turn in all his World War I medals and decorations. My aunt Malka's fiancé—yes, the queen had finally gotten engaged—was a lawyer but was no longer allowed to practice. Everyone had a friend or relative who lost his job because Jews were no longer permitted to have any public functions: teachers, notaries, bank employees, journalists, writers, actors, civil servants—all were purged from their jobs. Soon, it seemed no Jews were allowed to make a living in an establishment that wasn't Jewish and under German control.

One morning, a half hour after they left for school, Benjamin, Berel, and little Dvoirah returned home. Jewish children were no longer allowed to attend public schools.

My young aunt Dvoirah liked staying home, being with her mother, as did my uncle Berel, but my uncle Benjamin was heartbroken. He loved school. He had many friends there and enjoyed their rowdy games. He was a bright, clever, and good-natured student, an easy favorite of the teachers, and he loved the extra attention and spoiling he got from them.

In May 1942, a new ordinance was issued ordering all Jews to wear a yellow Magen David star, to be visible at all times on their clothing. My parents went to the AJB to buy them, for they had to be purchased. Their names were checked off a list. People whose names were not checked off ran the risks of coming to the attention of the German authorities. Not wearing the yellow star was a punishable offense: the threat of Breendonk prison incarceration was all too real.

The yellow star changed life drastically for its wearers; now their Jewishness was as physically obvious as if it gave them racial features. It marked them immediately as separate from the rest of the population and made them vulnerable to the different attitudes of passersby. Some jeered at Jews or pushed them off the sidewalk when they saw them; others looked at them with pity or sympathy, but most kept their eyes downcast when they walked past Jews, uncomfortable, pretending they hadn't notice that yellow badge of persecution.

My mother told me that one day, when she was dutifully wearing her yellow star on the lapel of her coat, she joined a long line of women queuing up for bread in front of a bakery in her neighborhood. Suddenly, the woman standing behind her shoved her out of the line; when my mother shoved back into it, the woman in front of her didn't let her stand behind her. And so it went; each time she tried to get back into the line, some woman pushed her away. Possessed by a determination she didn't know she had, my mother did not give up but butted back in line. When her turn came to be waited on, she went to the counter, placed her food stamps on it, and asked for her allotment of bread. The shopkeeper looked right through her and addressed the person behind her.

"It's my turn," insisted Golda. "I've been waiting like everyone else."

"I don't sell to Jews," said the shopkeeper. "Go away." The woman behind my mother shoved her and sent her reeling, but Golda did not lose her balance. The other women in line started laughing. Golda saw a Belgian policeman outside, standing on the sidewalk. She walked out of the shop and went right up to him, thinking that because he wasn't German he would listen to her. In her mind, he still represented Belgian law. She told him what had happened.

"I have a right to that bread like everyone else," she said. "I have a three-year-old child. We have to eat."

The policeman looked at her flushed cheeks, her bright eyes, and the yellow star on her coat.

"Come," he said, and, taking her arm, walked her back into the bakery, right up to the counter. Calling the shopkeeper, he said: "You give this lady her bread."

The woman quickly sold my mother the bread. The policeman declared in a voice loud enough for everyone in the shop to hear, that if my mother ever had any problems getting served in this shop, she was to come and tell him, as the police station was only two blocks away, and he would see to it that it would never happen again.

From that day on, no one shoved Golda out of line again in that shop. No one spoke to her, and the shopkeeper waited on her silently, eyes filled with hatred, but Golda always got her bread, and to her, that was all that mattered. She never forgot the incident: the humiliation the yellow star brought her, and the kindness of the policeman whose compassion was perhaps due to a foreboding that things would get a lot worse for those unlucky Jews.

BRUSSELS, 1942

The year 1942 was the turning point of persecution for the Belgian Jews; it was the beginning of the end. The AJB received orders to send large numbers of Jews for forced labor, first to the north of France, then to Germany and Poland. Since so many Jews were unemployed, the AJB thought it was the perfect solution. Families of men who volunteered were promised future privileges and immediate double food stamps. In spite of the rosy prospect of employment painted by the AJB, very few men volunteered, and the organization was forced to summon a certain number of people to be drafted for the work. This they did by turning to the registration ledgers and choosing among the names.

Mannes, my father's older brother, was among the first to be called. He was told he would be working for the Todt Company in the north of France for a few months, after which he would be sent home with a tidy sum of money. In spite of Mannes's reassurances, everyone was very upset to see him go, especially his father, whose health continued to deteriorate.

"God in Heaven, that we have come to this," he said, kissing his son good-bye. "This is the last time I'll ever see you: I won't survive this."

"What are you talking about?" asked Mannes. "I'll be back in a few months. Things will get better; you'll see." But the old man shook his head and wept.

He proved to be right; the image of Mannes boarding the train in Antwerp, his arms full of food packages his wife and mother had cooked for him, was the family's last glimpse of him—none of them ever saw him again.

My grandfather caught pneumonia and died of it in April 1942. Since Jewish burials were forbidden by then, there could be no religious ceremony. He was buried in an anonymous grave, in a civil cemetery, with only his children present, except for Mannes, who had not responded to the telegram that the AJB had promised to forward.

Golda wept for the father-in-law who had never accepted her as a daughter. She thought of her own father, who had died a day before my birth. She also wept for her sister Henna, whom she had not heard from in months. She was very worried about her: rumors about the extermination of Polish Jews abounded. Henna had never made it to Belgium; something always came up, and now, of course, it was too late. And could Golda even guarantee that her sister would be safe with her in Antwerp? And so Golda wept for her father-in-law, her own father, and Henna, her sister who at the age of ten had mothered her.

Later, much later, Golda learned that Henna, her husband, and child ended up in the Lodz ghetto with the other Jews of the surrounding Polish shtetls. Someone remembers seeing her being deported sometime in 1943; she was holding her little boy in her arms. Mother and son were probably gassed at Auschwitz, for there is no camp identification number for them, which means that they were selected for extermination as soon as they got off the train. Her husband died in Buchenwald.

My mother wanted to leave Antwerp and go to Brussels. Henna Wunderman and her family had done so and urged Golda to do the same.

"No one will know you in Brussels. You won't have to wear the yellow star all the time. And Moishe with his red hair, and Dori, who is blond! Believe me, no one could tell they're Jewish. In Antwerp, everyone knows you. Come to Brussels—we'll help you find a place," her cousin wrote to her.

Moishe was reluctant to leave his family. Now that his father was dead, it was just his mother at home with the three youngest children. Berel was almost sixteen and would never be bar mitzvahed. Little Dvoirah, as she was still called, was fourteen, and clever Benjamin, seventeen.

"We should really all stay together," Moishe said. "If we separate, how will we be in touch, how will we find one another?" He would have won the argument were it not the fact that soon afterward he himself was summoned to report for deportation to a work camp. By that time, stories had leaked out that their destinations in Germany and Poland were not labor camps, since the people who had left were never heard from again. Trust in the agency faded, and fewer and fewer people showed up when summoned.

"Don't go, please, don't go," Golda begged Moishe. "Let's move to Brussels. They won't find us there."

My father hesitated.

"What will happen to us if you go?" asked Golda. The time of promised double food rations and monetary rewards was over by now; one was simply told to report. "Think of your daughter," Golda continued, knowing that she was pulling the right string. No matter how attached Moishe was to his mother and siblings, now his little daughter, me, was what mattered most to him in life. From the beginning, he had worshipped the cranky baby who in turn responded to him as to no other person. My mother said that as an infant, I could recognize his step, and as soon as I heard him coming into the room, I would start bouncing in my crib and scream in delight until he came to pick me up in his arms. Unlike her, I forgave him his long absences, his other concerns, and would always drop whatever I was doing to run to him.

These stories of my father's attachment were very important to me when I was growing up after the war. My mother had created a sort of cocoon of our relationship that was to protect and separate me from the rest of the world. Although I was very happy to be reunited with her, at times her love felt stifling because it demanded total devotion and loyalty and meant sharing her pessimistic ideas. The confirmation of my father's love gave me a sense of normalcy for those years and a sense of escape from my mother's hold; it meant that there weren't just the two of us, but there had been another person attached to me and who, by his absence, made no demands.

Besides this, I knew that I looked like my father, and my mother often told me, when she was angry with me or disapproved of something I had done, that I was just like him. Her condemnation became a sort of alliance with my father. If I was like him, he was like me; I turned him into an idealized accomplice.

Meanwhile, the AJB summons frightened my father. For the first time, he seemed to realize the danger of the situation and the threat to his own family if he were to report as told. He agreed to leave Antwerp.

Keeping her word, Henna Wunderman found us an apartment in Brussels and arranged for a fictitious address.

"What you do," she explained, "is to register at an address but live somewhere else so no one knows where you are, and at your real address you don't wear the yellow star."

It was a ruse. The concierges of the "false" addresses were in on it. For certain sums of money paid at regular intervals, they would collect all official mail and act as if you were indeed living there.

Henna Wunderman knew a concierge at number 3, rue du Palais who would pretend we were tenants in the building there. "You're so lucky that Moishe doesn't look Jewish; believe me, no one will ever ask him for papers." And looking like him, I was so obviously his daughter that as long as he could pass for Christian, I would too. The apartment we would live in as a Christian family was on rue d'Aerschot; it had two rooms and was in a gentile neighborhood full of small shops. The landlords wouldn't ask questions because their son was married to a Jew.

Things were getting worse. The AJB was beginning to fall apart. Too many unconfirmed stories about death camps were circulating to be ignored. Some of the leaders of the organization had refused to continue turning people over to the Gestapo and had themselves been sent to the Breendonk, a German prison twelve miles south-west of Antwerp that preceded Malines as a transit camp for Jews who were to be shipped to concentration camps. The Germans took over the rounding up of Jews; only they didn't bother mailing summons to people. By using the Jewish registers, they simply showed up with paddy wagons and picked up whole families. There were also incidents of people arrested on the streets and hurled into wagons right then and there.

The news from Antwerp was terrible. Benjamin and little Dvoirah had been summoned by the AJB when it was still functioning in August, and their mother had let them go. Who knew where they were now? They had left together with their suitcases on the same train. Their mother and Berel had seen them off. My uncle Benjamin told me decades later that as soon as he and Dvoirah stepped off the train in Auschwitz, they were separated, and as she lined up with other women, she waved at him; that was the last he ever saw of her.

Now Moishe was very worried and felt guilty: he thought that he should have brought his family to Brussels with him.

"You couldn't have done that. How could we have hidden seven people? Where would we have put them? Besides, they wouldn't leave, remember? They wanted to stay in Antwerp so they could be with your sisters Ethel and Malka," my mother reminded him.

A few months after they had moved to Brussels, my mother and father had a surprise visitor: Mannes's wife, Moishe's sister-in-law, who showed up in tears.

"I had such a hard time finding you," she said to Moishe. "I'm also hiding in Brussels. I've heard from Mannes. Someone brought me a message: Mannes says that he is in Normandy, France, in a Todt factory camp. He can get out. One of the guards there lets people escape for money. There is someone here who knows all about it and will bring the money to Normandy; he gave me his name and his address. Moishe, I have the money, but I'm afraid to go. If something happens, who will take care of my little boy?" Needless to say, she had never received the money or double food-stamp rations that the Germans had promised when Mannes was first called.

"Don't worry, I'll go for you," said my father. "I'll take care of it."

Mannes's wife gave him the money and left. This time Golda could not talk my father out of going to meet the stranger and give him the money, no matter how much she pointed out the danger to him or used my safety as an argument. He felt too guilty about the deportation of Benjamin and Dvoirah not to rescue his brother Mannes. He left immediately to meet the man his sister-in-law had identified as the go-between her husband and the guard who could be bribed. He came back an hour later.

"Nothing to worry about," Moishe told my mother. "M. Holland, that is the man's name, has already gotten ten people out that way. He's a Catholic Belgian citizen, which is why he can travel to France. I'm to meet him in the waiting room of the Gare du Nord train station tomorrow at one p.m. with the money. He thinks Mannes will be freed in two days." Although Golda had an uneasy feeling about it, she didn't say anything. My father was happier that evening than he had been in months. He played with me for a while and then helped Golda with the dishes after supper.

He was still as cheerful the next day as he got ready to leave. My mother walked into the kitchen to see him button my coat on me.

"I thought I'd take Dori with me," he told her, and said that I would love the excitement of the train station; it had been such a long time since we had done something special together.

"Are you crazy," asked my mother, "taking the child with you on such an errand? My god, what if something happened?"

"Nothing's going to happen. You worry too much. But if it will make you feel better, I won't take her," said Moishe.

But I would have none of it and wouldn't let my mother remove my coat. I threw my arms around my father's legs and started screaming.

"Tell you what," he told me. "I'll be back so quickly, you don't even have to take off your coat. You stand by the window here and watch me leave in the street, and I'll turn around and wave at you. And before you know it, I'll be back and you'll wave at me again, and I'll come up and we'll go out together."

My mother told me that I stood as told, at the kitchen window from where I could see the street. My father soon appeared and waved at me with both hands, and then he was gone. According to my mother, I stayed by the window, and every time she tried to remove my coat, I started screaming, so she let me stand there dressed to go out.

The afternoon wore on and Moishe did not return. I brought some of my toys near the window and played there, but I still wouldn't let my mother take off my coat; it was as though as long as I kept wearing it, my father would come back to take me out, as he had promised. When night fell, Moishe still had not come back. I would not eat anything but started yawning and soon fell asleep on the floor by the window. My mother picked me up and carried me to bed, where she removed my shoes but did not take off my coat. She told herself that she didn't want to wake me and have me start screaming again, but in truth, she was so worried that she had begun to believe in the magic of the coat herself. As long as I wore it, Moishe would come back.

She told herself that he had run into someone he knew and had forgotten what time it was. *Just like Moishe to be so irresponsible*, she thought. Or maybe that person, M. Holland, knew someone who had important news and they had to wait for him. She thought of a dozen explanations for Moishe's absence, but she couldn't convince herself. She felt as though a cold iron hand had taken her heart in its grasp and was squeezing it.

By the next morning, my father still hadn't come back. My mother washed and fed me, and this time I let her take off my coat and even ate breakfast without a fuss, though usually a picky eater; I was probably hungry because of not having had dinner the night before.

My mother didn't know what to do. Where was Moishe? Should she go looking for him at the train station and ask around? What if the Gestapo was there? She was reluctant to take me with her, but she would not leave me alone in the apartment. She decided to go to Mannes's wife; perhaps she had heard something.

But Mannes's wife had heard nothing and looked extremely worried when Golda told her that Moishe had not come back from his meeting with M. Holland.

"Oh my god, oh my god," she kept on saying. She offered to keep me while Golda tried to find out what had happened, but my mother did not want to let me out of her sight.

"It's okay," she told the distraught woman. "I'll take Dori with me. I'll let you know if I hear anything, and you do the same." She was glad to leave, because the other woman had started to cry, and Golda did not want to cry, too, at this stage; she needed her strength. She went home and waited. By the next morning, she knew that the worst had happened. Moishe had never not come home at night, no matter what he was doing. And to not come home for two nights in a row meant that something bad had happened.

She dressed me, and we went out to rue du Palais, the "false" address my mother and father had written down on their registration papers. Maybe there was something there for her. As soon as she rang the bell and the concierge recognized her, the old woman pulled us into her apartment and quickly closed the door behind us.

She was very agitated. "You can't use this address anymore," she said. "Someone was here and left this envelope for you. Your husband has been arrested, and I'm sure the Gestapo are going to come now to look for you. What shall I tell them?"

Now that what she dreaded the most had happened, Golda found herself very calm. She tore open the envelope and read the letter, which was in Moishe's handwriting. He told her that he trusted the person carrying this message, and that he had been arrested at the train station. *It had been a trap*, thought Golda. *I had been right in not wanting him to go.* He told her not to worry, that everything would be all right. He asked her to send him his warm boots, his tallith, and a picture of me in care of the AJB agency on avenue Louise. He also told her to move right away as the Gestapo were bound to come looking for us at both addresses.

"Where should I go?" asked Golda out loud. The concierge looked very worried. "Not here, not here anymore," she replied. The letter was dated September 10, 1942.

"What shall I do if the Gestapo come looking for you? What shall I do?" asked the concierge.

"Just tell them that I left, that we moved a month ago and told you we were registering our change of address, and that you don't know where we went," answered Golda.

"Where will you go?" asked the concierge.

"Don't know. I think I'll go back to Antwerp," Golda replied, suddenly mistrustful.

My mother took me by the hand, and we went to Henna Wunderman's house.

"Oh my god, poor Moishe," Henna exclaimed when Golda told her what had happened. "What are you going to do? Stay with us awhile."

"No, I can't, I must stay in the apartment in case . . ." Golda started to reply when she was distracted by a loud fight between Simon and me. Simon was Henna's youngest son; only a year older than me, he was eleven years younger than his sister and twelve years younger than his brother, which made him as spoiled as an only child. We loved playing together, although we often fought because I was not used to sharing anything. Now we were both pulling at a red truck, and I suddenly hit Simon, who started to cry.

My mother became extremely angry. How could I be so selfish and fight over a toy when my father had been arrested by the Gestapo, and how could Moishe be so stubborn and not listen when she begged him not to go? Golda got angrier and angrier with him, and she started hitting me again and again. The next thing she remembered, Henna was holding her arms back, yelling at her to stop. My face was red with the marks of my mother's hand; I was trying to catch my breath. Simon had stopped crying but looked very frightened. Nathan, Henna's husband, had walked into the room and picked me up; I was now wailing and screaming, "Daddy, Daddy!" He held me in his arms and carried me out of the room. Simon went to hide his face in his mother's skirt, and Golda started crying. For the first time, she let herself go and cried and cried for her red-haired husband, Moishe, whom she would never see again.

BRUSSELS, 1982

It took me a while to find the Ministry of Public Health. Given the imposing name of the governmental office in the Belgian capital, I had expected shiny, bright, modern structures like the ones in big American cities; instead, it was a gray building in a circle of houses that looked like warehouse depots. The structure reminded me, once I stepped inside, of an old-fashioned bank that had been abandoned: heavy revolving doors, stone floors, counters with glass-sliding panes but no one behind them. The place seemed empty. I went back outside to double-check the number on the building. Could I be in the wrong place? No, the number was 31, and the plaque on the corner wall of the building read: "Square de l'Aviation." It was the address that Myriam and Esther had given me. I went back inside, yelled "hello," and heard someone coming—a white-haired woman wearing a heavy navy-blue cardigan. Although it was a typical hot July day, indoors it was quite cool. I had been so tense coming in that I hadn't notice I was shivering.

"May I help you?" she asked.

"Am I in the Ministry of Public Health?" I asked doubtfully.

"Yes, yes," she answered.

"I would like the section of the Civil Victims of the War." (That, I guessed, was the euphemism for "Jews.")

"Do you have an appointment?"

"Yes, Madame Aubrey is expecting me." She wasn't, but that was what Esther and Myriam advised me to say. Mme Aubrey was in charge of this department, and I had been assured that she would be very helpful.

"Just a moment," the woman said, picking up a telephone on a counter. "I'll tell her you're here. What is your name?" Given that Mme Aubrey had never heard of me, it would not be surprising if she refused to see me. I don't know what I would have done if that had happened. Would I have felt relieved in not having to face what was bound to be painful, or insist on seeing her, having come all this way? But Mme Aubrey apparently agreed to have me come up, since after hanging up the phone, the woman said: "I'll take you there."

I followed her through a maze-like series of corridors to wind up outdoors again, in a dark courtyard. The walls of the buildings circling it were black with dust and grime. There were pigeons flying about, and their droppings littered the ground. In the middle of the courtyard stood an old-fashioned elevator shaft topped by a gallery whose door opened as we approached.

"Just press the ninth-floor button. Madame Aubrey will be waiting for you," the woman said.

I did as I was told, and when the elevator stopped and its door opened, a smiling woman was waiting for me in the gallery connecting it with the building. I had expected Mme Aubrey to be an old woman who resembled the decrepit appearance of the buildings, and I was surprised at her attractive, youthful appearance; she was friendlier than the woman downstairs, who had made me feel like I was imposing on her.

"You wanted to see me?" she asked.

I told her that Myriam and Esther had given me her name in America, and that I had come to find out about my family during the war.

"We used to live in Brussels. We were Jewish," I added redundantly.

"Yes," she said. "We have placed all the information we have in files arranged alphabetically. Come with me," she said. Her friendliness had changed into an expression of warm sympathy and support that I was grateful for, as it relieved some of my tension. The rooms we went through were stark; they looked like old stacks in university libraries, the kind that no one consults anymore—rooms full of dust, books yellowing on the half-empty shelves. We stopped in one such room, where there was a long wooden table whose corners had been reinforced with metal. Two bare lightbulbs hung from the ceiling. Mme Aubrey turned on the lights, and then went to the green metal file cabinets standing against the wall.

"What was your family's name?" she asked.

When I told her, she said, "Lots of Katzes," as she pulled out the K drawer. I saw that it was full of yellowing manila folders. Would one of them really be mine? I still couldn't believe that it would be this simple. "Katz what?" she asked.

I told her that my father's name had been Moishe Chaim, and my mother was Golda. She pulled out two files, one very thin and the other thick. The thick one was labeled with my father's name. "Here you are," she said.

Just like that! I was amazed. After all these years of not knowing what had happened, of fantasizing all sorts of outcomes, two sleeping files were here waiting to clear up the mysteries. I felt a mixture of guilt and incredulity; guilt that I hadn't come earlier, and incredulity that the files had been there all along. I still thought it must be a mistake, that the files were not of my parents, or at least that they wouldn't reveal anything I didn't know.

"I also have a box of small objects from Jews who were deported," Mme Aubrey said after I told her that my father had been deported. "We can look to see if there is something that belonged to your father," she added, while pulling out a large cardboard box filled with tagged objects from a nearby cupboard. We looked through the eyeglasses, empty wallets, keys, cigarette cases, notebooks, letters, et cetera that were lying there. I held high hopes that I would find something that had belonged to my father, some personal object that would connect me to him; something concrete that I could touch, which would make him materialize for me. Such personal objects play an insignificant role in "normal" circumstances and would have been discarded, but these had not been normal circumstances. So they had been collected and kept, perhaps as evidence of the existence of their dead owners. But there was nothing in the box that had belonged to my father: not only had he been robbed of the years he would have lived after the war, but nothing remained of the years he lived before the war—it was as though he had been erased.

"Would you like to see your own file?" Mme Aubrey asked, interrupting my train of thought.

Since I had been only a year old when the Germans invaded Belgium, I didn't think there would be a file for me. "Even if you were only one week old," she went on, "there would be a file for you. Everyone had to be registered. What is your name?"

"Dori," I started to say, then caught myself and replied, "Astrid Katz."

She pulled out another manila folder and gave it to me. I sat down at the long table with the three folders, overwhelmed. I started to open my mother's folder, which held only a couple of forms and cards, mostly in German.

"The Germans wrote these?" I asked.

"Of course, they were fanatical record keepers. When they invaded Belgium, everyone had to register at city hall, which they controlled, and had to fill out many forms to receive the right identification papers," she explained.

It had never dawned on me until now that when one country occupies another, everyone must be accounted for; no one could remain anonymous. Everyone had to have an identity card listing his name, address, religion, race, and profession. Other cards needed were ration cards, work permits, travel papers, and so on. And those were the days not only before computers, but also before electric typewriters. Since the Germans controlled all civic offices, post offices, city halls, and other local governmental establishments, they had access to all the registers. One couldn't budge without papers; they had to be shown constantly to a German soldier or official or a Belgian policeman. Jews were identified by their cards, so that they could be treated differently from the rest of the population.

I had decided to start with my mother's folder because I thought it would hold the least surprises because I knew, more or less, what happened to her during the war. Her registration card listed her name, her parents' names, her husband's name, her address, and her profession: seamstress. Her religion was written as "none," but her race said "Jewish." According to the Germans, Judaism was not considered a religion but a race, which meant that all Jews were atheists. Her identity card was like her registration card except that it had the word "JUDE" (Jew) in capitals stamped on it.

"Duplicates of these documents were kept by the Gestapo," explained Mme Aubrey. "When they decided to arrest and deport people, they just went to the files, chose cards, and sent Gestapo men and vans to the addresses listed."

It was all cut-and-dried and efficiently simple, although not everything listed on the cards was true. My mother did not live at the address stated on the form but somewhere else, where she was not registered. After 1942 she did not carry the identity card stamped "JUDE" across it anymore, but a false one that imitated the real one. It gave her a different name, other parents, a Belgian birthplace, a Catholic religion, and her race was stated as white.

Thousands of such fake papers had been created by underground resistance groups, some Jewish, some not. Perhaps that ability to forge important documents was responsible for saving more Jewish lives than other forms of resistance. I suppose these counterfeit papers, like those of my mother, worked because the German or Belgian officials who examined them were not always conscientious, sometimes took short cuts, or were inattentive, impatient, or bribable—in other words, human. They did not always scrutinize the cards carefully and at times would let rather crude imitations get by. On the other hand, sometimes people with the best-forged papers were caught and deported. It was mostly a matter of luck. Luck worked for my mother. Whenever she was asked to show her papers, they were accepted as valid. She was young, pretty, and spoke Flemish without an accent. Maybe the German or Belgian officials stopping her gave her figure more attention than her card; did she ever flirt with them to divert their attention? She was very careful, of course, but mostly she was lucky.

I turned to my own file next, amazed that as a small child, I had been considered important enough to be tracked and have my own surveillance. I opened the folder to find a form that said, in German, that I was a three-year-old atheist (my age at the time of this registration), without profession, and without nationality, since my father did not have Belgian citizenship and in Belgium nationality depended on that of the father. If the Germans had come to the address registered in Brussels, they would not have found me since I was hiding with the Walschots in Beersel. Although I knew, of course, how I had survived the war, for the first time I think I really felt in a visceral way the kind of danger I had been in and what "hiding" meant. Suddenly I thought, *My god, I could have been killed*, and was amazed at my own luck. It could have been me on one of those awful trains speeding toward a concentration camp. I had been too young to understand and be afraid then, but now I realized that I might not have existed: a strange fear took hold of me for a moment.

Mme Aubrey explained that these archives existed because after the war the Belgium government had requested that all papers pertaining to Jews who lived in Belgium during the Holocaust be turned over to it. Some of these German documents in the files had been given by the Polish Red Cross and other organizations that had helped "clean up" concentration camps after they had been liberated. A library of some sort had been set up in Brussels, and various resistance organizations, rescue groups, and allied departments had turned over their own papers to complete the documentation. My own file also included all the information pertaining to my having been hidden by the Comité de Défense des Juifs (CDJ), the resistance group that saved children during the war. Afterward, Mme Aubrey showed me the three books, in another file cabinet, turned over by that organization. One book carried the real names of the children and codes for their hiding places; another book listed codes for the children and named the hiding places, and the third book was the connection between the other two, all in code. Only three people in the organization had access to all three books. Just as I had felt the threat of extermination for the first time, I now felt surprise at all the work and effort of strangers to save a child like me. I was listed as code number 343.

The people who hid me did not know my real name or my mother's or her address in Brussels. Neither did the woman who had brought me to their home. She and my mother had met in a railroad station. Had she been caught, she would not have been able to say whom she had hidden. If the Gestapo had come to the Walschots, they would not find a Jewish child, but Astrid Von der Laar, the daughter of their Catholic Belgian niece, who, with her husband, had volunteered for a work camp in Germany; the Walschots had the papers to prove it.

This is how I was able to confirm what Myriam and Esther had told me about the Walschots, the family who had taken me in. In those three books, I found the codes for the places I was hidden. The first was in Beersel with the Walschots. The date of placement, February 9, 1943, and the payment for my room and board were also noted: the Walschots received thirty francs per day for me. Of course, there was no documentation about the risks and danger they ran in hiding me.

The second number, 727, referred to the home in La Hulpe, where I had been placed on January 16, 1945. Although I remembered the orphanage very well, I had no recollection of my arrival there at the age of five and a half. After leaving the Walschots, I had been reunited with my mother for a short time; I think I expected life to become normal again, but that couldn't happen since "normal" for me meant life with my own family. Although we didn't know it at the time, by then my father was dying on a march from Auschwitz into the Polish woods; my fantasies about him showing up one day, surprising us, would have been impossible to realize.

I had left the most difficult file, my father's, for last. He was the one I knew least about, and I had wanted to prepare myself gradually for what it could reveal by reading the other two first. I reached for it now, but Mme Aubrey told me that it was lunchtime and that she was obliged to close the office until 2:30 in the afternoon. She was sorry she couldn't just leave me alone; it was the rule. She would put all the papers on her desk and lock her office. I could come back in a couple of hours, and they would be waiting for me. I left, finding my way down the elevator, across the dark courtyard, through the maze of corridors, and into the room that resembled an old-fashioned bank lobby. The white-haired woman in the blue sweater was waiting by the door. She locked it behind me. I stepped outside, stunned by the bright daylight. How could the sun still shine? I started walking. I don't know how long I walked. I was in a daze and looked at the pedestrians and the street life in amazement. I couldn't connect the world I had just read about with the world around me, yet they were separated only by time. I went into a café and ordered a sandwich but could not bring myself to eat it.

As soon as it was 2:30, I was back to the Ministry and went through the same routine with the white-haired woman wearing the blue cardigan sweater. "Yes, Madame Aubrey is expecting me"; this time I knew the way, and indeed she was waiting for me by the elevator door. We went straight to the table where the files were. Again, there was no one else in the room. I sat down and opened my father's file. Mme Aubrey remained discreetly in the background as she had in the morning. She seemed to sense when I was about to ask a question and would be nearby, or when I would start crying and wanted to be alone; then she would somehow disappear.

My father's file contained index cards, sheets of paper, a few photographs, and other forms in various sizes; some had been filled out by the Germans, some by various organizations my mother and I had visited after the war when we were trying to find out what had happened to him or if by chance he was still alive somewhere. There was his identity card, stamped "JUDE" like that of my mother. He was not only an atheist of the Jewish race, but he was also a "bastard," at least that was what his card said. My grandfather, an ultra-orthodox-practicing Jew, had been married to my grandmother by a rabbi but had not undergone a civil ceremony, an occurrence not uncommon with Jews in Czechoslovakia back in those days. The Germans did not recognize this kind of marriage, therefore my father was illegitimate in their eyes.

There wasn't much information about what happened to him in the years after his arrest, but the little there was, was specific. One of the "official" cards stated that he had been arrested by the Reichssicherheitshauptamt, the internal security police, on September 10, 1942, on the street. Then he had been sent to the Dossin Casern in Malines, the processing center in Belgium where Jews who had been arrested went through registration and clearing before being sent to Germany and then on to Poland to various concentration camps. He had been deported from Malines, as Esther had written to me, on Convoy No. 9, in train car no. 291, two days after his arrest. (Several months later, back in the United States, I read about Convoy No. 9 in Maxime Steinberg's book *Le dossier Bruxelles-Auschwitz*, which lists records of those trains and convoys. It had taken a thousand people: 398 men, 390 women, and 212 children; a child was anyone under sixteen. After the war, 29 of those people came back, about 3 percent. So my father's chances of surviving his ordeal had been very small.) Convoy No. 9 first stopped in Kosel, Germany, where a sorting took place. I knew that some people were selected for extermination right away; there were no more papers concerning them, nor were they given a number to be tattooed on their wrists. This is what happened later to my uncle Fischel, his wife, Rachel, and their fifteen-year-old son, Abraham.

My father apparently was one of the "lucky" ones chosen for slave labor rather than immediate extermination. Here, the information was confusing. He had first been sent to Blechhammer, a branch of

Auschwitz. It was a synthetic gasoline plant named Oberschlesische Hydrierwerk A.G. As I read on, I wondered what he did there. What gave him hope to endure? He must have been worried about us; we had no news of him then, and he certainly had no news of us. He didn't know if we had been arrested like him or if we had escaped. He had always had much faith in my mother's resourcefulness and cleverness: I am hoping that he believed in them enough to expect that we were safe and that it gave him a strong reason to try to survive.

Then he had been transported to Feldafing, a commando of Dachau, working for the firm Hochtief A.G. It was a small concentration camp with only forty prisoners. I learned this from a directory, which Mme Aubrey showed me afterward, compiled by the Allies after the war: *The International Tracing Service Catalogue of Camps and Prisons in Germany and German-Occupied Territories, September 1, 1939–May 8, 1945.* It is a very thick book. Besides the main concentration camps, I read, there were many branches, called "commandos," some large, some so small they had as few as only nine prisoners. I wondered where the Germans got the personnel to run all of these? Where did they get the guards, the sentries, the directors, the clerks, the drivers, and so on?

"Oh, they had plenty of help," Mme Aubrey explained. "First of all, there were thousands of collaborators in the occupied countries. The Germans did not have to search far to find Poles, Austrians, Hungarian, Rumanians, and others to do the job; some were very eager. Then there were all the Germans prisoners who had been in jails before the war and who were now transferred there: criminals, murderers, crooks—people not trustworthy enough to serve in the German army, but certainly good enough to serve in the camps. They became the guards, the hated *Kapos*, the executioners . . ."

All these strangers eager to be part of the machinery to kill my father! The room seemed to have darkened suddenly, or was it simply the passing of the afternoon that had chased the light away? My heart pounding now, I went on reading the file. Such seemingly innocuous, dry material. Name, address, birthplace, and so on;

the forms could have been applications for a driver's license, travel visa, or hunting permit, rather than formalities involved in killing millions of people.

I came upon the Auschwitz document about five in the afternoon. Here it was, a form filled out to admit my father to the main camp on April 1, 1944, April Fools' Day, a year and a half after his arrest. When I saw the date, I thought, *What irony!* And furthermore, the camp would be liberated in less than ten months, and the war would be over in about a year and a half. If only he could have lasted longer. Of course, my father had no way of knowing that. The admission form was in German, and I read it as well as I could, but a few months later, when I was home, I went to consult a German colleague, to make sure I had understood it correctly; I had.

As a heading, it listed the camp: Auschwitz; the type of admission: Jew; and my father's identification number: 177679, which had been tattooed on his arm in Kosel. He no longer had a name; he was no longer considered a person. The questions were printed, and the answers were written by fountain pen in a script that must have earned its writer a high mark in penmanship in school. Right away, what seemed a harmless question elicited a confusing answer. First and family names, it asked. The pen answered: "Mozes Katz" and "Israel." I learned that all Jewish men were called Israel by the Germans; all Jewish women were referred to as Sarah.

It went on routinely: birthplace and date, address, and name of parents. Here, besides the name of my grandmother, the clerk had written "bastard." After religion: none. After race: Jewish. After property: none. Then there was a physical description. Height: 1.62m. I learned, for the first time, that my father was very short; only two inches taller than me, and I am five feet two inches. I don't know why learning of his short stature touched me so; perhaps it made him seem more boyish and vulnerable. He had red hair, blue eyes, and sixteen missing teeth. I wondered if they had made him open his mouth to count his teeth. Under "weight," they had simply put "thin," which he always had been, according to my mother, but I doubt that after spending almost two years in camps, he could have been anything but "thin." The form continued with a description of his nose, his mouth, and his ears; these were supposed to identify race. This was the man who had waved at me when I was three standing by the kitchen window in 1942, watching him walk away down the street. How could it be the same person?

I was surprised by the number of languages he spoke: Czech, Hungarian, German, and Flemish. Of course, Yiddish hadn't been listed; that didn't count as a language, nor did Hebrew, which he also knew.

Criminal record, political affiliation, underground membership— all these were answered by "allegedly none." Then, at the bottom of the document, there was the oath, which paraphrased read: "I am hereby informed of what my punishment will be if I have given any false information or should any of the above turn out to be untrue." A very shaky hand had signed: *Mozes Katz*. Under "Der Lager Kommandant," the camp director had flourished something illegible.

It seemed that my search for my father had ended here, with those two signatures. That was all the archives would give me, but they had given me the reality of the person who was my father, and that, in spite of his terrible fate, filled me with a strange comfort. He no longer seemed some sort of fiction my mother had invented to explain my birth, but now he was a flesh-and-blood person whose last years were chronicled and recorded on a piece of official paper. Here was proof that he had really existed! Throughout my childhood in Belgium, I had felt abnormal because I had only one parent; I had a hole in my life, a lack I couldn't define that made me less of a person. But now, because of these documents, I believed in the actuality of the man, and this meant that, like everyone else, I had had a father. Now something hard inside me started to melt; I felt the pain of being connected to what had happened to him.

My father had been in Auschwitz for about ten months when it was liberated by the Russians, on January 25, 1945, but it was impossible to tell from these documents if he was still alive by then. It was so painful to think that he almost made it, but then time was measured differently in concentration camps; ten months might have seemed an eternity. A few years later, in San Francisco, a visit to man who had been there with him gave me some of the details of his last days, but here in this folder, there was nothing but the finality of the papers; no death certificate, just a notation of his disappearance on subsequent forms filled out when my mother and I tried to trace him.

There had been a few small identification photographs in my father's file, taken probably before his arrest. They showed a high forehead, a bony, angular face cut through by a mustache, and beautiful, big, dreamy eyes: he was around thirty. I asked Mme Aubrey if I could have the photographs, as I had no other pictures of my father except for that of his engagement and wedding. She said that nothing was allowed to be removed from those files, however, seeing how disappointed I looked, she said she suddenly remembered that she had an urgent phone call to make in her office, so if I would excuse her for a few minutes . . . I detached the pictures while she was gone, careful not to tear the papers they were glued to, and put them in my wallet.

I left the Ministry of Public Health in a daze. I took a cab back to the apartment Myriam and Esther had lent me for my stay in Brussels. I sat on an art deco white leather sofa, facing a big picture window on the fifth floor of a modern building, and stared at the sky for hours. I had been in Belgium for only three days looking for family who had been strangers to me all these intervening years, and in three days I had crossed forty years. I had found Beersel, the house I hid in, and Martin, the oldest of the Walschot children. The youngest child, Jeanne, who had been my war sister, was waiting for me in Waterloo. I had visited La Hulpe and seen the grounds of the orphanage that had been my private inferno turned into a quiet, serene retreat for nuns.

I had gone into a tall, dark building, and I had disturbed my father's grave. Instead of a skeleton in a coffin, I had found official papers that were already fading, already yellowing. What had I learned from all this? I felt burned out, as though I had walked through a curtain of fire. I thought of *As If It Were Yesterday*, the film that had started my search. I remembered seeing Andrée Guelin in it, the woman who had organized the network of hiding places for Jewish children in Brussels and who had been the go-between for hundreds of cases. I remembered how she spoke in the film, wearing sunglasses that hid her eyes, her gray hair flat against her head. "The most difficult thing," she had said, "was taking the child from its parents. They were so frightened. You couldn't tell them where you were taking their son or daughter, what your name was, how they could reach you. The parents were desperate. All of them had already seen relatives and friends arrested and disappear. Some of them had lost a wife, or a husband, or another child. It was very difficult to witness their pain at parting with their child. They were thinking that perhaps they would never see each other again, and for most of them, this was indeed the very last time they would be together."

A list of names and phone numbers had been left for me in the kitchen of the apartment; names of people who might help, Myriam had said. I looked for Andrée Guelin's number, and when I found it, dialed it. I didn't know why I was calling her, but her face had seemed so kind in the film. Perhaps she could tell me something more.

A pleasant cheerful voice answered the phone. We talked for a while after I told her why I called. She asked if I was staying long in Brussels.

"No," I answered, "just until tomorrow." Well, perhaps we could meet some other time, she suggested. I was bound to visit Brussels again. To find out if she was the one who took me into hiding, she asked me my name.

"Astrid Katz," I told her, "but I was hidden under Astrid Von der Laar."

"Just a minute," she said. "I'll check in my book." She was back on the phone after a few seconds. Did she keep that book by the telephone, within reach, like an address book? Perhaps people called her all the time now, asking for information, since seeing her in the film.

When I confirmed that I was born in Antwerp, on July 13, 1939, she said, "Yes, I was the one who took you into hiding. You might be interested to know that afterward, I wrote down by your name, 'a ravishing little girl.'" I hung up the telephone, went back to the white art deco couch, and cried for a long time.

The next day, I packed my bag and left Belgium by train. When I landed at the Gare du Nord in Paris, the station was very crowded. As I walked toward the entrance of the Métro subway, I was jostled. I looked at my purse; it had been opened, and my wallet with the photos of my father was gone. I stood in line for hours to report the theft to the security guards at the station, then I went to report it at police headquarters. I spent the next few days queuing up at various official lost-and-found departments of the city, and I went, several times, to the Bureau of Public Transportation. I filed forms with the American embassy. I looked for those photographs as I had looked for my father, but after a while, it was obvious that they were lost to me forever. Later, if it had not been for the photocopy of the Auschwitz document that Mme Aubrey sent me, I would have felt that I had imagined those files. I had really found my father, but then I lost him all over again.

CLOSE CALLS, 1942

"Don't ask how I managed after your father's arrest," said Golda. "We went to my brother Fischel, and we stayed there for a while. I was afraid to go back to the apartment, and yet I thought, *What if I am not there, and Moishe sends a message?* You started acting up; you wouldn't eat, got cranky, were often crying, and I lost patience with you. Somehow, life went on." Somehow, indeed! My mother's resourcefulness in those times amazes me, but she was very vague when I pressed her for details on how she survived, telling me, "You did what you had to do" or "Don't ask."

Although she was very worried about my father, she was also angry with him for trying to rescue his brother Mannes when she had begged him not to go, had told him that it was too dangerous. She would often tell me after the war that she felt he cared more about his family than his wife and daughter, and that if he had listened to her, maybe he wouldn't have been caught. I don't know if I believed her, but as a child, I often felt that my father had abandoned me—a feeling I tried to counteract with her stories of how much he had loved me, how I had been the most important thing in his life. Then why did he leave? It wasn't perhaps until I read his German file in Brussels, forty years after the war, that I really understood that he bore no responsibility for what had happened, that he had been caught because he was a loving man who would not let his brother down.

As the weeks went by after my father disappeared, my mother couldn't stop thinking about what was happening in Antwerp. She thought she still had old friends there and wanted to be comforted by them and by whoever remained of Moishe's family. She knew that Benjamin and little Dvoirah had been deported, but she wondered how the others were faring. Finally, she couldn't stand not knowing, so she decided we would go to Antwerp to see everyone, that is, whoever was left. Mostly, I think she wanted them to see me—that I was all right, and that she was taking care of me. She had heard nothing from my father since that first letter, although she went to the Jewish agency every day for news. She had sent him packages: his boots, his tallith, a muffler, some gloves, socks, chocolate, and coffee. And a picture of me that she had had taken by a professional photographer, in part to show him that I was doing well. (I still have that photograph, where I look surprisingly like a normal, happy three-year-old until you notice that for all the formal, plush settings of the studio, my shoes are scuffed and dirty, and my dress looks mended.) I know now that he never got any of the things that were sent to him. Who did get them? Was it the German officials or the agency members? "Jews themselves," my mother told me. "They took themselves very seriously, very proud of their important positions, but when the Germans closed the agency, they were sent to the camps, like everyone else."

Anyway, my mother decided to go to Antwerp. Her brother Fischel was against it; he thought it was too dangerous for us to travel, but my mother had made up her mind. Of course, she couldn't call ahead. No one had a telephone in those days, and she was afraid to write to announce our arrival. What if the mail were intercepted and read? She knew where to find what was left of Moishe's family: they would be at home. Where would they go with all the curfews for Jews in force by then? It was worse in Antwerp than in Brussels. In Antwerp, which had the second largest Jewish population in Belgium at the time, most Jews lived in one neighborhood so that they would be easily contained and identified; they all wore the yellow star. My mother would have to wear it there herself; she was too well known not to.

So she did what she always did when she went to city hall for our allotment of ration stamps; she sewed the star on the lapel of her coat but didn't wear the coat. She carried it folded on her arm, the star on the inside so that nobody could see it. She felt safe that way; if she were stopped, she could always show the lapel of the coat to prove that she was obeying the law. She would put on the coat once we reached Antwerp. Luckily, the weather was still warm, and she didn't have to wear it as we went to the train station.

We took the train from the Gare du Nord. For once, my mother told me, I was behaving, excited to be on the train, looking at everyone; then seated on her lap, my face pressed against the window, licking the glass, I made patterns with my fingers in the dirt. My mother let me; eventually I fell asleep. The compartment was full. She gave the conductor her ticket and her false identification card; the one that didn't say "JUDE" on it because Jews by then were no longer allowed to travel in Belgium. She had used her false ID card, the one Henna Wunderman had given her to buy the train ticket. At the time she didn't know where Henna got it; later when Golda learned about the resistance groups that were helping Jews, she found out about the counterfeiting units, and she often made use of forged papers.

Just before we pulled into the train station in Antwerp, the train went over a loop on a bridge in the middle of a neighborhood. Golda could see, out of the compartment window, people wearing the yellow star, lined up. There were German soldiers around them and vans waiting. They looked as if they had thrown their belongings together in piles on the ground. There were suitcases, packages clumsily tied with strings, blankets and pillows and eiderdowns, some boxes with pots and pans. There were babies crying and children running up and down the lines, and non-Jews—that is, people without stars—watching from windows and doorsteps; a few of them waved as the lines of people started to move toward the waiting vans.

My mother was very frightened. Nobody in the compartment

said anything, although they had all seen what was happening. A middle-aged woman kept wetting her lips and was staring at me hard, which made my mother nervous. A few minutes later, we pulled into the station. We were the last people to leave the compartment because we had been sitting at the opposite end of the exit door. Golda deliberately took her time so that no one would see her put on her coat. But the woman who had kept staring at me also seemed to be stalling to get off the train. Finally, because Golda couldn't delay any longer, she put on her coat with the yellow star, picked up the few packages she had brought, and grabbed my hand; we left the compartment and started walking down the train corridor. The woman was in front of us; she stopped abruptly, turned around, and walked up to us.

"Don't get off," she said. "It's not safe for you. I take this train every other day, and for the last four times, the Gestapo were here by the exit door. Twice they arrested Jews right on the spot. Don't get off this train. And take off your coat; I saw your star on it. Go back to Brussels; you can buy your ticket on the train, right from the inspector."

She put her hand on my head and then moved on and got off the train without looking back. My mother didn't know what to do. She had bought all these gifts at great cost, and she really wanted to see everyone in Antwerp; she was homesick for that city, and it would be comforting to see old friends. Then she remembered the line of Jews being marched into the vans. She turned around, and we went back to our compartment and took our same seat, then waited for the train to start again for Brussels.

"Today, I know that woman saved our lives," my mother said. Of course, had we gotten off the train in Antwerp, we would not have seen many people. Benjamin and little Dvoirah had been deported weeks earlier. Moishe's father had died in April. Maybe Moishe's mother was still around: no one knows when she was deported or what happened to Berel. The sisters and their husbands and children had all been arrested. In any case, we never saw any of them again except for my uncle Benjamin, who survived Auschwitz. The others were all killed; perhaps some of them were already dead at the time of that aborted trip to Antwerp.

"Life was constant anxiety after that," my mother went on. Fischel found us a new place to stay on chaussée d'Etterbeek, not far from where he lived. It was a three-room apartment in a house owned by an elderly couple whose son had been in the Belgian army and died at the beginning of the war. They had a notion store on the ground floor: needles, threads, lace, buttons—those sort of things. There was a kitchen and a "salon" behind the shop, and a couple of rooms on the second floor. We had the third floor to ourselves. Our apartment had a big bedroom, a decent-size living room with a balcony overlooking the street, a coal stove for heat and cooking, and a small narrow kitchen with a sink and a gas hot plate. Of course, no hot water; you had to heat that yourself. There was a toilet between the first and second floors for everyone to use; the landlady kept it immaculately clean. In wintertime, she would wrap the toilet in blankets to prevent the water from freezing since there was no heat in the small room; it seemed to work. I remember the place well, because after the war we stayed in that apartment until we left for America in 1952. The landlady became very attached to me, often greeting me when I came home from school with a sweet and a warning to be good. She might have known by then that we were Jewish, but it didn't matter to her because I was "her" little Astrid; I think she had known all along but had never let on.

"I gave the Rogerses, that was their name, my false identification card and told them my husband had volunteered for a work camp in order to make money. Your blond hair and blue eyes made my story convincing," my mother told me.

Meanwhile, she needed money desperately and couldn't find work. Henna Wunderman helped out again. She knew an old Jewish couple, the Zuckerbroads, who needed a place to stay. Their two sons had been deported, and they had fled their apartment afterward. They had money; they would pay our rent. My mother gave them the bedroom and told the Rogers they were her parents from Poland who did not speak Flemish or French. The Zuckerbroads did speak Polish, but mostly they spoke Yiddish, which Golda asked them not to speak whenever anyone was around. They had no papers, so they couldn't leave the house. My mother did all the shopping for them, but every now and then Madame Zuckerbroad insisted on doing it herself. She said she would go crazy if she didn't get out the house once in a while. Or she needed to buy some things herself, since my mother didn't buy exactly what she wanted.

They would go out late at night, my mother and Mme Zuckerbroad, who wore a hat with a veil that she would pull over her face. A big black coat with a fox wrapped around her neck was her usual outfit. My mother thought that Mme Zuckerbroad was more conspicuous in that hat than if she had just shown her face.

Mme Zuckerbroad spoke a few words of Flemish; they were from Antwerp, but my mother begged her to speak as little as possible and to let her do the talking. "I understood her need to get out, poor woman," my mother said, "but I was very scared then and tried hard to talk her out of these outings."

During the day, the couple slept a lot. Monsieur Zuckerbroad read the same books over and over; his wife sewed or knitted but mostly wept, kissing the photographs of her two sons who had been arrested on the street. "God knows what will happen to them. God knows when they'll come back," she kept on saying. She was right; they never came back.

The Zuckerbroads stayed with us until the war ended. Their money helped, but it wasn't easy to have three adults and a small child in that apartment. My mother had to do a lot for them since she was the only one who could really go out. At times she resented it, feeling like their servant. My mother lost touch with them after the liberation; neither she nor they wanted to continue a relationship formed at the bleakest time of their lives.

I was a problem. My mother needed to find work and didn't have any place to leave me. The Zuckerbroads were no help. They paid no attention to me, too worried about their own problems. Besides, it wasn't safe. There were stories that if people were arrested with children, they would all be killed.

Henna Wunderman came to the rescue again. She told my mother about the underground resistance groups that hid Jewish children. They found Gentiles in the countryside who took children into their homes, pretending that they were relatives. You had to pay room and board, but the Committee for the Defense of the Jews, one of the clandestine groups that dedicated itself to saving Jewish children, would pay it.

As 1942 had been the year that the arrests and deportation of Jews intensified, it was also the time that the resistance to the Germans increased. Perhaps because of the German defeat at Stalingrad, the Germans no longer seemed invincible; the occupation might perhaps not last forever. Whereas resisting had seemed a hopeless, brave, and perhaps slightly absurd gesture before, now it seemed to make more sense in view of the eventuality of the enemy's defeat. The ranks of the underground fighting groups grew. People who had tried to remain "neutral" began to choose the fighting side; some who had collaborated even became active opponents to the regime. Therefore the irony of 1942 was that life for Jews became more dangerous, but there was more help and hope for them. My mother was told over and over again that it was possible to hide me and that she should do so.

"Dori will be safe, and you'll be safer without her," Cousin Henna told her. "You can get work without worrying about her. Everyone who can is trying to hide their children." She said that she was hiding her own children. Her daughter, Bella, was going to a convent in a week; her son Max was placed in an asylum for tuberculosis patients; and Simon, her youngest, had been put in a home for blind children. Fischel also thought it was a good idea to hide me. He was devastated by the loss of his daughter, pretty Leah, who had been one of the first people called by the AJB at a time when no one realized how dangerous it was. That was a year ago, and he hadn't heard from Leah since taking his leave of her, on avenue Louise, at the AJB address. The AJB had no news and no longer tried to reassure him that everything would be all right.

"Think of the child first," Fischel told my mother. "You know it's best for her. If something happens to you, at least she can survive. And, if something happens to her, you have a chance."

"I won't survive if she is taken," my mother told him. "Dori has become my whole reason for living. I have no one but her. Who knows if I will ever see Moishe again?" She felt bad as soon as she thought that, but she had such a sinking feeling in the pit of her stomach when she thought of my father. And her family in Poland? Her father was dead, and she was pretty sure that her sister had been taken; if not, she would have heard from her by now. Her brother Fischel, his wife and son, and her cousin Henna were her only family now, along with me. She couldn't stand the idea of something happening to me and not being able to do anything about it. She didn't want us to be separated, and she really didn't trust anyone, especially Gentiles. How could she be sure that the people who hid me would not turn me over to the Gestapo for money? How could she be sure they would treat me well?

"Believe me, these will be trustworthy people," said Henna. "They were especially chosen for that; the resistance knows them. You have got to hide Dori."

But my mother couldn't bring herself to do it; she just couldn't give me up.

One day, my mother told me, as she was doing the old trick with the yellow star on the lapel of her coat, taking it off as she and I came out of the municipal building where she had gotten her ration of stamps, she saw a German soldier looking at me very hard. She started walking away fast, but he followed us. Finally he caught up with us, stopped us, and asked: "Are you Jews?"

My mother blurted out, "No, of course not, do we look like Jews?" He looked at me, then said: "Let's see your ID papers."

My mother said that she then snapped; instead of being afraid, she became very angry and belligerent.

"Why?" she said. "Why do you have to bother Belgian citizens all the time? I haven't done anything."

"Are you Belgians?" he asked.

"Yes, of course," she said, afraid to open her purse because she had her real ID card in it that said "JUDE" in big red letters; she had needed it to get the ration stamps. She held her coat tightly against her.

"What's the matter, forgot your papers at home?" he asked, while he kept looking at me.

"No," she said. "I don't know why you have to see them."

My mother remembers him as being young, slightly fat. He looked like a kid playing at being a soldier, which made him seem harmless; perhaps that was why she could keep up the pretense of not being Jewish. He squatted down to my height.

"What's your name?" he asked. I didn't answer but stepped back, hiding my face against my mother's skirt.

"What's your name, pretty little girl?" he asked again. My mother was afraid that I would lapse into Yiddish but I didn't, although I looked like I was going to cry.

"She's very shy," my mother said.

"Yes, I can tell," he said. "I also have a little girl her age, and she's very shy too, just like yours. Well, all right," he went on. "Go ahead, but don't go down this street. At the end of it, there is a passage where they are arresting Jews. I know you're not Jewish, but I would not go there if I were you."

My mother didn't say anything but took my hand and turned around. She didn't know if this was a trap, but we walked away. How had he guessed, she wondered.

"Astrid," I suddenly yelled at him, turning around as my mother dragged me along. "Astrid, Astrid." She had taught me to say that my name was Astrid if anyone asked.

That night my mother walked over to Henna Wunderman's house and told her that she had decided to put me into hiding. Henna said she would talk to the right people and that in a few days someone would contact her.

Two days later, a young woman rang our doorbell. She did not introduce herself. She and my mother talked for a while, then the woman said that another woman would take me into hiding the next day. (This was to be Andrée Guelin, whom I had spoken to on the phone in Brussels. I saw her again, more than forty years later, in New York, at a conference on the hidden child. She had become a kind of celebrity because she had helped hide hundreds of children; TV cameras recording the event had followed her around. When I approached her and identified myself, she put her arms around me and wouldn't let go for a long time, pointing at the cameras and then proudly at me, saying, "One of my children, now a college professor!") My mother hadn't expected my going into hiding to happen so soon, but the woman said it had to be done right away. She explained, in a few words, how we were going to proceed and then left.

That evening my mother packed a small suitcase for me, putting in lots of warm clothing, some food, and a few toys. She couldn't sleep all night. Was she doing the right thing? Would I be safe? Would she ever see me again? What was going to happen? Were they going to treat me well? How would she know? If something happened to her, then what would happen to me? How would she find me again? She told herself a dozen times that she simply wouldn't show up the next day at the meeting place. She knew they would understand if she changed her mind; they couldn't force her to give up her own child. Yet, in her heart of hearts, she knew she had to do it; she knew we were in greater danger together than apart.

At four o'clock in the morning, she woke me up and started to dress me. The night before, she had tried to prepare me by telling me that we were going to be separated for a little while. I was going to live with nice people, but I mustn't tell anyone I'm Jewish. I had to be good, do what they told me, and she would come and get me very soon. I am not sure I understood, but I did not raise any objections. Now that it was time to leave, I kept asking questions and telling her over and over that I didn't want to go. My mother told me to be quiet so as not to wake the Zuckerbroads in the next room. She had told them nothing, not that she didn't trust them, but because it was easier not to discuss it with them. Golda knew they would start crying about their own children. She put my hat and gloves on me and my new winter coat, the one I had refused to take off after waving at my father from the kitchen window the day he was arrested. I was three and a half years old.

"I carried you downstairs, with the little suitcase," my mother told me. "I opened the front door very quietly and shut it quickly behind me. It was still dark out, but the sky was streaked with graying bands and there was light in the distance. I started walking toward the train station, as I had been directed to do. Madame Andrée was waiting for us at the Gare du Midi. She was standing in front of the entrance that led to the ticket counter. She came up to me and kissed me on both cheeks as though we were old friends and said in a loud voice, 'How nice to see you, and thank you for bringing Astrid back. Did you enjoy her visit?'

"'Yes,' I answered, 'she was very well behaved.'

"Madame Andrée took the little suitcase and started to take your hand, but you refused and grabbed hold of my coat," my mother went on. "She pried your hand open and picked you up. I turned around and walked away. You started crying; I could hear you screaming, 'Momma, Momma.' I just walked away as fast as I could without running and did not turn around. I thought that if I did, I would collapse or I would go back and take you from that woman's arms.

"I circled the train station, went in, crossed the waiting room, and went into the public bathroom. At the entrance, I gave the custodian at the counter some money, and she gave me some paper and said, "Stall number three." I went into stall number three and locked the door behind me. Putting my hand over my mouth so as to muffle my cries, I put my head against the wall and sobbed like I had never sobbed before or since. I just couldn't stop. It was as though I was being dragged into a black hole and couldn't fight it. I was afraid the custodian would hear me, get suspicious, and come knock on the stall. Then I thought that I would never see you again, that I had just given my child away to an agent of the Gestapo, and that they were going to kill you. I don't think that I've ever been that afraid in my life.

"After a while I wiped my eyes and my face with the paper the custodian had given me and flushed it down the toilet.

"The custodian said nothing when I came out of the stall. She barely looked at me. After all, train stations are places of departures, separations. Perhaps these scenes of grief happened all the time. It could have been lovesickness. I was still young enough for that, twenty-nine. My married life ended at twenty-nine: I have been a widow ever since."

My mother went on to say that she doesn't remember the rest of that day. She probably went to her brother's house. She spent the next couple of weeks in a daze. She must have cried a lot, worried, regretted her action. Fischel and her cousin Henna kept telling her that everything would be all right. Poor Fischel, his hair had turned white from worrying about Leah, his daughter.

My mother had to tell the Zuckerbroads that she had placed me in hiding and that she didn't know where I was. When she did, Mme Zuckerbroad looked frightened.

"How could you do that? Give your own child away? If my sons were here, you would have had to hack off my arms before I let them go," she said, and went on and on with recriminations. But for once, M. Zuckerbroad spoke up and told her to be quiet. Then giving my mother's shoulder a little squeeze, he told her she had done the right thing.

ASTRID AND DORI IN HIDING, 1943

When Father brought my birth certificate home from city hall four days after I was born, my mother was very surprised.

"Astrid! What kind of a name is that?" she asked when he told her how he had registered me.

"A Christian name," he answered, explaining why he couldn't choose Dvoirah, the name they had agreed upon, because the registry clerk refused to accept it. So he named me after a queen. But it didn't matter, he assured her, since they would always call me Dvoirah, Dorele, or Dori. Astrid would be my outside name, the one for ration cards, residence permit, and police visits.

And so it was that there were two of us from the beginning. I'm sure I was not aware at first that I had another identity, since no one paid any attention to Astrid. Mother and Father, Uncle Fischel, pretty Leah, Benjamin, Henna, Malka—everyone made a fuss over Dori.

For my mother, Astrid did not exist most of the time, but sometimes she would call me by that name when people who only spoke Flemish would come to visit, and she would have to answer a lot of questions. At times I was a little confused.

"How old is Astrid?" the Flemish people would ask.

"Does Astrid have any brothers and sisters?"

"Did you file papers for Astrid?"

"Where is Astrid's father?"

Even though Mother was only pretending that Astrid was her daughter when we had to go to offices and fill out forms, I would get scared, start crying, and wet myself. Mother would get angry and spank me before cleaning up the mess.

Then one day, Mother said she was sending me away to live with some nice people for a while. She had to, she said, because she had to hide me. There were bad people all around where we lived who would do terrible things to us if they caught us because we were Jewish.

"They will send you to a very bad place, if they find you," she said.

"What about you?" I asked.

She said, "I'm also going to hide."

"Why can't we hide together?" I asked.

"It's better if you hide in one place and I hide in another. It will be harder for them to find us both that way."

"I don't care," I said. "I want to stay here with you."

"You can't," Mother answered. "You have to be a big girl now, not a baby, and you have to do what I say." Then she took me in her arms and kissed me. "Mamele," she said, "it is only for a little while. When it's all over, I'll come get you, and we'll all be together again."

"Father too?" I asked.

"Yes," she said, and repeated that we had to hide because we are Jewish and that I had to pretend I was Astrid.

"Because Astrid is not Jewish," Mother said, "but you know that you're not really Astrid, and you must never forget that you are Jewish. Only you can't tell anyone, no one; it's our big secret."

The next morning, when Mother woke me, it was very cold in the apartment. She was dressed already and had lipstick on, which meant that she was going out. There was a suitcase on the floor.

"Where are you going?" I asked.

"We're going out," she said. "We're going to hide you today. Remember how we talked about it yesterday?"

"I don't want to," I said, as if I hadn't agreed yesterday, but Mother ignored my protests.

We went down the stairs very quietly. Outside, it was dark, cold, and windy. The streetlights were still on.

"Where are we going?" I asked again, this time meaning both of us.

"You'll see," Mother said, carrying me down the stairs. Our footsteps sounded very loud on the pavement. I thought they would wake up all the houses in the street, but they didn't. We went to a train station.

"*Shepsie,*" Mother said, "a lady is going to come and take you to live with very nice people. I will come to visit you soon and bring you many presents. You won't have to stay there long, remember."

I don't know if that mollified me or if I asked: "How many presents?" Before Mother could have answered me, a lady with dark glasses had come up to us. She and Mother talked, saying what a good little girl Astrid had been, then the lady bent down and picked me up and started carrying me away.

"Momma, Momma," I screamed, kicking at the lady. But Mother was walking away very fast and did not turn around. The sound of her heels on the train platform was like someone knocking on doors farther and farther in the distance.

The lady carried us to another platform, and then we were in a train going very fast.

"Look at the nice trees," said the lady, sitting by the window with me on her lap. "Look at the field, Astrid. Look at the red car."

I didn't care, but perhaps I was looking. I didn't say anything for a long time because I was very scared, but I was staring at everyone in the compartment, until a man asked me what my name was.

"Astrid," I answered, and then said, "Three," when he asked how old I was.

"What pretty blond curls," he said, and gave me a piece of chocolate. I didn't think I wanted any, but I grabbed it anyway and started eating it, so that I had to say thank you.

The people the lady brought me to were very old. The woman had gray hair and was fat, and the man had a mustache. "This is Astrid," said the lady, pushing me toward them; no one mentioned Dori.

"We're glad you're here," the fat woman said. Astrid let them pick her up and kiss her, although I hadn't wanted them to. There was also a girl with black braids, looking at us from behind the fat woman.

"Say hello to our daughter Jeanne. She'll be your big sister; she's fourteen," the woman said, and pushed the girl forward.

"Hello," Jeanne said, and smiled.

Astrid didn't say anything, but I said, "My father went away, but when he comes back, he is going to bring me many, many presents."

They all looked at me in surprise.

"She speaks only Yiddish," the lady who brought me explained, "but she will learn Flemish very quickly, you'll see."

I didn't want to stay, but the lady put my suitcase down and left without waving good-bye.

"My name is Régine but call me Mama Gine, and this is Papa Franz," the fat woman said, pointing to the man with a mustache.

I knew then that Mother had left me forever, that she had gone to be with Father, and that they were never coming back. I started crying, but Mama Gine paid no attention. She picked me up, calling me her little Astrid, turned off the light, took me to bed, and left me alone in the dark.

The next morning, everyone continued to fuss over Astrid. I realized then that from now on there would always be two of us. I had cried all night, but every time Mama Gine came into the room to look, she saw only Astrid sleeping and left as though she hadn't heard me. Even Jeanne, who slept in the same room, must not have heard me because she didn't wake up and ask, "What's the matter, Dori?"

Astrid and I had both wet the bed, but I felt like a bad little girl.

"It's to be expected," said Mama Gine. "First night away from home."

"I'm sure she's toilet trained," said Papa Franz. "They usually are at three."

"Astrid," said Jeanne, "next time you have to make pee-pee, use the potty under the bed. See the big, nice potty, just for you."

Astrid and I both nodded.

"You're going to be a brave little girl," Jeanne, Papa Franz, and Mama Gine told me.

But I didn't want to be brave. I wanted to go home, to be with Mother and Father. Astrid beamed with pride at the compliment. She didn't care that Mother wasn't here. She let them pick her up and hold her, but I kicked and screamed.

"She's so moody, so unpredictable," Mama Gine said. "One minute you can hold her; the next, she starts kicking and screaming."

"Better go easy for a while," said Papa Franz.

So they stopped picking us up, but soon Astrid sat on Papa Franz's lap the way I had on Father's and put her head against his shoulder and her arms around his neck.

Of course, she only did it so they would like her and be nice to her and not yell at her for wetting the bed, which we did night after night, in spite of the pretty potty. Mama Gine did not get angry.

Jeanne also liked Astrid best because every time I opened my mouth, everyone would say, "Shh . . . don't speak Yiddish. You're not supposed to be Jewish, remember?" But I didn't know any other way to speak. Astrid did: she learned Flemish and began to speak for both of us.

"Ask them when Mother is coming to get us," I told her, but she wouldn't.

"Ask them," but she kept on saying no, and I started crying; Jeanne came running, asking Astrid if she had hurt herself. She really hadn't, but since I kept on crying, Jeanne let Astrid play with her hair, braid it, and put ribbons in it like the ribbons in my hair on special occasions.

Mother used to love my hair. She would take hours combing it out after washing it, brushing strands around her finger to make them curl, then she would kiss each curl and call me her treasure.

I wonder if Mother misses me, I thought.

"Or remembers us," said Astrid. "Maybe she'll be like Father, who forgot us."

"It's not true," I said, but last night when I tried to think of Father, I couldn't see his face. I think that he is mad at me because I can't remember what he looks like. He turned his back on me.

"Daddy, Daddy, please turn around," I said. "Please come back. I'll be good, I promise." But he didn't move, so I yelled and yelled very loudly so he could hear me, and he came and picked me up and said, "Shh . . . little one, everything will be all right." It was dark and I couldn't see, but he smelled differently. He had a mustache that scratched when he kissed me. When he called me "Astrid," I knew that it wasn't Father; it was Papa Franz. I wanted my real daddy, so I kept on crying until I fell asleep.

The next night I tried again, but this time I yelled for Father very softly so Papa Franz wouldn't hear me, but Father didn't hear me, either. Astrid says he has another daughter, and he and Mother are together with her.

One day Mama Gine said to us, "Guess what? Your mother is coming to see you today, so you have to be extra good."

"Am I going home?" I asked, very excited.

"No, you're not, but your mother is coming all the way to see you. So first, let's get you very clean for your mommy."

I went into the kitchen with her, where a big pot of hot water was boiling on the stove. I took off my clothes, even though it wasn't time for bed, and Mama Gine washed me and dressed me in the skirt and blouse I usually wore to church on Sundays. Jeanne put a white ribbon in my hair to make me look pretty. Then Mama Gine made me sit down and eat some boiled potatoes and sausage. I really wasn't hungry and didn't want to eat, but Mama Gine said that I had to be good because my mother was coming. But then I thought, *What if it wasn't my real mother who was coming, the way Papa Franz had come pretending to be my father? Maybe this was a trick? I was supposed to be hiding so no one would know where I was. Maybe Mother was just checking up on me to make sure that I was keeping my promise?*

"I don't want her to come," I told Mama Gine. "I'm being good. I don't want to see her."

"Don't be silly, Astrid," said Mama Gine. "Of course you want to see your mother. You're very lucky that she is coming."

When I finished eating, Mama Gine said that it was time to go meet my mother but that it was a big, big secret and I must not tell anyone. Jeanne was going to take me. We left the house. Jeanne was quiet and holding my hand tightly, so tightly it hurt. I tried to pull it away, but she pulled it back, yelling, "Come on, Astrid, be good."

My stomach hurt. It was Astrid's fault. She ate too much. We walked down the main street toward the end of town, past the mechanic shop where the owner was standing in the doorway.

"Hi, Jeanne," he said. "Hi, Astrid. How nice you look with that big ribbon. What's the occasion? Going to meet a boyfriend?" And he started laughing. I wanted to tell him that I was going to meet my mother, but then I remembered that it was a secret.

"We're going visiting," said Jeanne, pulling me along fast until we seemed to be running. I told Jeanne I was tired; she picked me up and carried me. We stopped in front of the electric shop. I knew the place. It was Uncle Martin's shop. I had been there many times. Uncle Martin was Jeanne's brother, but that seemed strange because he looked almost as old as Papa Franz and was a daddy himself. Astrid and I sometimes played with his little girl, Catherine.

We pushed the door open and went into the shop. The bell jingled and Uncle Martin came in through the back door that was hidden by a curtain.

"Where is my mother?" I asked.

"Well, I haven't got her in my pocket," he said. "But if you'll give Uncle Martin a kiss, maybe she'll walk right in through that door."

He picked me up and said, "Come on, little heartbreaker, give

Uncle Martin a big kiss." But I started screaming, and Jeanne said, "Put her down, Martin. You're upsetting her." And taking my hand, she led me through the back door, across a courtyard, and into a shed, where she and I sometimes played. It was filled with open boxes of things that Uncle Martin sold. He always told us not to touch anything, but we did.

There was a bench. Jeanne and I sat down on it. Jeanne said, "Listen, your mother is going to be right here. I am going to wait for you in the shop."

"No, no, don't go," I said.

"Remember the song Papa Franz taught you Sunday, the one about the little bird being free?" she asked.

I remembered.

"Well, just sing it three times, and before you finish, your mother will be here. Come on, start!" And she got up and left.

I wasn't going to sing, but I could see Astrid opening her mouth and I didn't want her to start before me, so I sang: "*Vogel, Vogel frei . . .*" The bell in the shop sounded. I got up and hid behind the bench. A lady came into the room with Uncle Martin. She was wearing high heels, a hat and lipstick, and a dark fur around her shoulders. I had never seen her before.

Uncle Martin yelled, "Astrid, Astrid! Look who's here. Where are you—come out of hiding," and he came and pulled me from behind the bench.

"Here she is," he said to the lady, and walked out of the room. The lady looked at me, then picked me up and held me very tightly and starting crying.

"Oh my god, my god," she said. "Don't you recognize your mommy?"

I said no, but I was also crying. The lady's smell was nice, and it reminded me of something; it made me feel I was somewhere else, and I liked it.

"Mamele, mamele," the lady said. "I am so happy to see you. Mommy missed you very much." I felt as though something hard was melting inside, and it hurt and felt good at the same time.

"*Ich will gein aheim*," I said without thinking. *I want to go home.*

"Oh, I'm so happy you still speak Yiddish," she said. "You haven't forgotten."

She sat down on the bench and took me on her lap and kissed and hugged me. I played with the eyes of the fox fur around her neck.

Mother asked: "Do they spank you a lot?"

"Yes," I answered, "when I make pee-pee in bed." It wasn't true, but I thought if I said that, she would take me home.

"Look, Mommy bought you some good food," she said, and began to take things out of her bag. "Here's an orange. Eat it right now," she said.

"I don't want to," I said. "I want sausage."

"Here," she said. "I also brought you some chocolate, but first you have to eat the orange, then you can have the chocolate," and she started to peel the orange, squirting juice on her fur. I ate the orange, and a piece of chicken, and then some of the chocolate. She put the rest in the pockets of my skirt.

"This is for later, but don't tell anybody. Mommy brought it only for you. Hide it."

"I want to go home with you," I said. "I don't want to hide anymore. I don't want to be Astrid. I want to go home with you."

"Mommy can't take you with her," she said. "I have to hide like you. Remember you are Jewish."

"Why can't we just not be Jewish and not hide anymore?" I asked.

"You're too young to understand, *shepsele*, but you have to do what Mommy says, and you must not forget what she told you. Now tell me what I told you."

I started saying it. We had rehearsed it so many times before I went into hiding. I knew it by heart: Daddy's name, Mommy's name, my real name. ". . . daughter of Moishe Chaim and Golda Dychtwald Katz. I am Jewish. Please take me to 27 chaussée d'Etterbeek to Fischel Dychtwald."

"No, not that address anymore. Now you must say, 'Please take me to the Jewish Agency.' Uncle Fischel is not there anymore."

"Where is he?" I asked.

"Who knows, God only knows," she said. I was afraid she was going to cry again. I couldn't remember Uncle Fischel.

"Don't you remember Uncle Fischel?" Mommy asked. "He always gave you raisins and carried you on his shoulders."

Yes, now I remembered Uncle Fischel. He smelled of cigarettes (or was that Daddy?), and he was bald, and he would let me rub his bald head "for good luck," he said, when I rode on his shoulders.

Mommy said she had to go, but I didn't want her to.

"I want to go home with you," I said again.

"Now, *shepsie*, Mommy told you, you can't. You have to be good or Mommy won't come see you anymore."

But I wasn't good and started crying. "I don't want to stay here, I don't want to stay here."

Uncle Martin came into the shed and said, "You better go now or you will miss your train." Mommy got up.

"No," I said, and started pulling at her skirt; I was being very bad, but I didn't care. Uncle Martin picked me up, and Mother ran out of the room, leaving that nice smell behind her.

Jeanne carried me back home, where Mama Gine took me on her lap and stroked my hair.

"Now, tell me," she asked, "how was your visit with your mother?"

I wasn't going to say anything, but right away Astrid piped out: "Mother gave me chocolates for me alone. None for Jeanne and none for Papa Franza and none for you."

"Now, let's see," Mama Gine said. "Let's see what's in your pockets."

Astrid took out the chocolates and put them in Mama Gine's hands.

Mama Gine said, "I'm sure you want to share with Jeanne. She shares everything with you. We all do; you are one of the family. Now, you don't want to be selfish, do you?"

I really did want to be selfish, but Astrid went on: "Mother brought food, lots and lots of food, and I ate it all. Chicken and oranges and chocolate."

"Did you, now—after that big lunch you ate, you still had room for all that?" Astrid made a face. She was getting even for Mother's visit, because Mother had ignored her the whole time.

"Well, your mother thinks we don't feed you enough, but then she doesn't realize how much we love you here. What a lucky little girl you are, to have two mothers."

Before I could stop her, Astrid yelled out, "Mama Gine, Mama Gine. I love only Mama Gine. I don't want to see Mother anymore. I don't want her to come again. I'm not Jewish, I'm not Jewish. I love Mama Gine and Papa Franz and Jeanne."

"Shh . . . shh . . . ," said Mama Gine. "Don't get so excited. Of course, you are one of us, but you have to be a good little girl and listen to what Mama Gine says."

Later that evening, Papa Franz taught me a new Flemish song about a lamb getting lost then being found again. We all ate the chocolates after supper, for dessert. Astrid asked for two pieces, but I found them hard to swallow.

When we were in bed, I couldn't fall asleep. I felt terrible about the things Astrid had said, especially about liking Mama Gine best. I knew Mother would be mad at me.

"I'm very mad at you," Mother said, now standing by my bed in the dark. "You're a bad little girl. I don't love you anymore. I'm going away with Daddy without you." She and Daddy, who suddenly appeared, turned their backs on me and started walking away. At first, I was very surprised to see Daddy. I hadn't seen him for a very long time. I recognized the white suit he was wearing. He had worn it many times before, especially on Shabbat. His red hair shone so much, it looked as if he were on fire. I suddenly wanted very much to be with him.

"Daddy, don't go!" I yelled. "Don't go! I'll be good, I promise." I ran after him and put my arms around his legs, but they felt empty. He turned around very slowly, and I saw that his face was missing. He bent down to pick me up.

"What happened?" asked Mama Gine.

"She threw up," said Papa Franz. "Better get some towels. Her head is burning. I think she has a fever."

"It's because her mother came; now she will be sick for days. It is too much for the child. Maybe we should tell her mother not to come again."

"Come on, Régine," said Papa Franz. "How can we ask the woman not to come see her child? She must be worried sick all the time."

"Well, it's not good for her; it really upsets Astrid," said Mama Gine. "Besides," she continued, "I'm not sure it's such a good idea for her to come here. This is a very small village; people notice things, and the Germans are right down the street."

"Don't be silly," said Papa Franz. "Nobody would talk."

"No, not on purpose," said Mama Gine, "but still. The other day the mechanic asked me who that good-looking woman was who spent all afternoon in Martin's shop. One of his paramours?"

"Well, let him think so. With Martin's reputation, it's easy for Jacques to think that."

Mama Gine said, "I'll ask Madame Andrée not to bring her for a while. It's too dangerous."

I don't know what else they said because I fell asleep in Papa Franz's arms.

I like Papa Franz best. He is nice to me, and even though he calls me Astrid, I know that he knows that I am really Dori, and that he likes me better than Astrid. Only he is not supposed to say so.

For Jeanne, it makes no difference if it's Astrid or me. She is always ready to play whatever game I want, and she takes us everywhere with her, even to church on Sunday. I like church. It smells good, and there is music, and the windows are so pretty, full of colors with pictures of pretty ladies and their little babies. I don't like having to sit still for so long, but after we kneel on straw chairs, Astrid shows Jeanne the pretty patterns on her legs, like flowers or spiderwebs. Jeanne always carries us when we are tired, and she lets us pull on her braids like bells, as long as we don't pull too hard.

I think Mama Gine likes only Astrid. She listens to her, she never hears when I say something, and she always takes Astrid's side. But then, Astrid tells her everything, everything about Mother and Father, and Uncle Fischel and everybody, and how we lived. She always tells on me too. Whenever I want to keep a secret, Astrid tells it to Mama Gine, just to spite me or maybe to make Mama Gine like her best. She told Mama Gine that I buried food in the yard because I didn't like it, and that I let the rabbit out of the cage because Jeanne said we were going to eat him.

Actually, I don't really mind that Mama Gine likes Astrid best. Sometimes when I think that she is being nice to me, it makes me think of Mother, and it makes me feel very sad. Then I'm always glad that Astrid is the one who gets the kisses and the hugs. It lets me hide, and I can think of Mother so that she won't forget me.

I let Astrid do all the talking now. It's just easier. Everyone knows her already. She always knows what to say, what to do. This way I don't have to pretend all the time. Besides, she does a lot of things better than me. She's less scared. Yesterday, when the Germans came to visit and Papa Franz took us to the attic and told us to be very quiet and wait for him to come get us before coming downstairs, I was really scared. Astrid wasn't; she went to look at the soldiers through the crack in the door.

We do all the work together, me and Astrid. We watch over the sheep in the prairie and tell Mama Gine if they run away. We feed the rabbits. I love to stroke their fur. We feed the chickens. I hate that. They're mean. You have to go up to them, your apron full of seeds, and yell: "Here, chickee, chickee, chickee . . ."

Then they come running at you, very angry, trying to scratch your eyes out. I run away, and Astrid calls me scaredy-cat.

Now that the apple trees are full of flowers, Astrid and I sit under them banging a pot to make lots of noise so that the birds won't come and peck at the flowers, because when they do that, Mama Gine says that there won't be any apples. We bang and bang all afternoon, and the flower petals fall like snow. My arms get tired before Astrid's, but then I sing the song that Papa Franz taught us, the one about the bird flying free, wherever he wants:

"*Vogel, vogel frei . . .*"

Mother hasn't come for a long time now, but Astrid hasn't told anyone that I am Jewish. She doesn't tease me as much about it as she used to, not that she has forgotten, but I think she is afraid of making Mother too angry. Oh, yes, I know that Astrid wants to go home just as much as I do; she doesn't want to stay here alone. Sometimes I get a little confused and wonder if I am not Astrid, because everyone treats me as though I am. It would be easier to just let go of myself and be her. But then I think of Mother, and I know she wouldn't come anymore if I became Astrid, because whenever she came, she never said: "Hello, Astrid, how have you been?" And Astrid never got any kisses and hugs from her, and that made her sad. We know that when Mother comes, it will be for Dori.

JEANNE, 1983

Jeanne wrote to me first. I had carried her address in my wallet for months after my visit with her brother, Martin, intending to write her but hadn't yet done so. Her letter on pale blue stationery came from Waterloo—a small town that is an hour and a half by train from Brussels and is the site of Napoleon's defeat—where she lives with her husband. She is a grandmother now with a daughter living across the street from her, which means she sees her grandchildren every day. Her letter started: "Chère Astrid." How strange to be called Astrid again after so many years. It was a warm, affectionate letter written to someone she still called her little sister, but it was read by a grown-up woman she had never met.

I was five years old when my mother came to Beersel to fetch me home after the Allies landed; that was the last time Jeanne and I had seen each other. She hadn't forgotten me, Jeanne said, had always wondered what had happened to me all these years after the war; she hadn't known that I had emigrated to America until her brother told her of my visit when she got back in September from her vacation in Spain. She included in her letter a photograph of herself and her husband taken at some celebratory occasion, judging from his shirt and tie and the camera he was carrying. I didn't recognize the fourteen-year-old girl with long, dark braids I half remembered from my childhood in the heavy, bespectacled dressed-up matron in a beige fur jacket and long blue skirt. Her smile seemed shy and her face kind.

She asked me to come see her the next time I was in Europe. There was plenty of room, and I could stay with her. They had a house, a garden. Marcel, her husband, was eager to meet me; he had heard so much about me. (In fact, he was the one writing the letter because Jeanne felt her handwriting was not good enough.) I was touched by her eagerness to contact me as soon as she got my address. I had meant to write to her myself when I got back to the United States. I am not sure why I hadn't; on the one hand, I had been so excited at the prospect of connecting with the daughter of the people who had hidden me during the war. On the other hand, I had found Belgium so changed, so alien to my memories, I was no longer sure I wanted to revisit those childhood years that meeting her would force me to do. I don't know why I was ambivalent. After all, I owed her family a debt so large I could never repay it; the least I could do would be to show my gratitude by reconnecting with their daughter. Was I so hesitant because deep down, in spite of my gratitude, I harbored some of the negative feelings toward them that my mother had expressed? Or did I have such an idealized picture of the people who saved my life that the Walschots could not have lived up to it? In spite of my ambivalence, I was very happy to hear from Jeanne.

I answered Jeanne's letter, included a snapshot of myself, and asked her to tell me as many things as she could remember about those years, about her parents, about our life together. We started a slow correspondence, which was a little constrained on my part but not on hers. I wrote about my job, how my mother and I came to America, the weather, and other such superficialities. She wrote about how happy she had been to have me live with her family during the war; we had had great fun together. Those had not really been horrible years, and she would be happy to answer all my questions, but I must come and visit her: it would be easier to talk in person, and she would be so happy to see me.

While I was staying in Paris a year after receiving Jeanne's first letter, I went to Brussels to see her. I had declined her offer to pick me up at the Gare du Midi train station when I arrived from Paris or to put me up during my stay in Belgium. I was trying to make our meeting as easy and casual as possible, not sure how much time I wanted to spend with her. I didn't want to have to play the role of a grateful guest obliged to follow her host's agenda—more gratitude added to my debt; mostly, I wanted to be in control of the visit. After all, she was a stranger, and what did we have in common besides the year and a half spent together during the war? In fact, even in Paris, I still had not been sure I wanted to come; perhaps my mother had been right, after all.

So, Marcel and Jeanne came to pick me up in Brussels at the house of friend of a friend where I was staying, with Jeanne holding her one-year-old grandson in her arms. We were all smiles, except for little Nicholas, who was fretting and didn't want to be held. Jeanne looked just like her photograph and was wearing the same fur jacket, indicating that this, too, was a grand occasion. I couldn't quite believe this was the Jeanne of my memories. I put my arms around her, and we hugged and kissed, then stared and stared at each other. Were it not for the photo, I would never have recognized her, but she claimed that she had not needed my photo to recognize me; the same eyes, the same curly hair, even though now it was dark brown, and the same face I had at three. Perhaps because she was eleven years older than I, her memory of that time was better. The discrepancy between the woman hugging me and the young girl I remembered made it hard for me to believe that this was really my Jeanne.

We exchanged pleasantries: Did I have a good flight? Yes. Was the weather as bad in America as in Brussels? Yes. Did I find Belgium very changed? Yes and no. We left to drive to her house in Waterloo, a town I had visited as a child during my elementary school field trips to the grounds of that famous battle with its monument to Napoleon's defeat. I didn't see the stone lion of the British victory on a hill this time, only shopping mall after shopping mall on the road to her house. We stopped at a big "American" *supermarché* for last-minute items for the meal she was preparing in my honor. (The market, which seemed to also be a hardware and department store, was bigger than any supermarket I have ever seen in the United States.) Did I like chocolate cake? I don't but said yes to be polite, and later, after lunch, had to eat an enormous piece as my just deserts for lying.

When we reached their small white two-story house, Jeanne and Marcel took me out to the garden and showed me around a sparklingly clean house that smelled of furniture polish. They took me to the "guest room" they had just finished, working on it all last week because they had assumed I would be staying with them; I felt a pinch of guilt for having refused their hospitality. The living room was full of vases, artificial flowers, souvenir statues and ashtrays from their travels, and large framed family photographs on every wall; I was surprised and touched that my snapshot was there too. The photograph that caught my eye, however, was that of Jeanne's father. For a brief moment, I felt that Papa Franz was smiling at me personally, and that I was back sitting on his lap while he sang Flemish songs in a booming off-key voice. He always made me laugh. Then the moment passed, and I felt I had lost something; he was just a stranger again with piercing eyes and a big mustache.

Jeanne showed me her workroom. The windows looked out on the garden; there was a big sewing machine in the middle, and there were stacks of red leather purses and belts on the floor.

"I work at home," she said. "I sew these straps on the purses, then finish the seams. I work for a Jew. Strange that since the war, I have had so much to do with Jews all the time. Maybe because of the work I do. I work with leather, and Jews run the fine leather-craft business in Belgium, and this work suits me because I can watch over little Nicholas while my daughter works during the day; she is a schoolteacher. You will meet her and her daughter, Aurore, when they come home for lunch. Aurore goes to the same school where her mother teaches; it's right around the corner."

The remark about "Jews" made me uncomfortable at first. The war had been over for decades, so why still this need to identify someone that way? Did she still think of me primarily as a "Jew"? But how could she not, since it was my Jewishness that had brought me into her life? And, as she spoke, the distinction between Jews and Christians seemed inoffensive. She had spent her whole adult life near Beersel, where she was born and raised, and to her, the people she worked for were different from her relatives, her friends, and her acquaintances, in part because they were "Jews." If she made the distinction, it was not out of dislike or envy or hostility; it was a way of describing the man who owned the leather business. Or so I told myself.

"The man I work for is the president of the Union of Deported Belgian Jews. I told him about you, and he would very much like to meet you. I have to deliver all those purses, and I thought I could take you with me," she said, stroking one of the red purses lying near the sewing machine. "I stayed up until three this morning to finish everything so that I could be free to spend the whole day with you." The pinch of guilt returned; I had the foreboding that I was not the warm and grateful person I felt I should be on this occasion or whom she had perhaps expected; so much effort on her part to spend time with me while I had been so ambivalent about our meeting.

Maurice Pioro, Jeanne's "Jewish" boss, turned out to be a rather important personage. When we met later that afternoon, he showed me photographs of himself and Eisenhower and celebrities. A survivor of the concentration camp Dachau, he was very active in Jewish affairs pertaining to the Holocaust. He looked up my father's name in a directory he kept right in his desk drawer. He told me what I already knew: the date of my father's deportation, the number of the convoy and of the train that took him to Auschwitz. But he also told me about the monument erected in the center of Brussels, a memorial to Jews deported from Belgium.

"Your father's name is on one of the walls," he said. I told him I would go there because I wanted to find not only my father's name but also that of his brothers, Berel, Mannes, Joseph, and Benjamin; and his sisters, Ethel, Malka, and Dvoirah; and their wives and husbands; and my five cousins. I might also find there the names of my mother's brother, Fischel, his wife, Rachel, and two children, Leah and Abraham.

After leaving M. Pioro, Marcel and Jeanne drove me to the monument. We walked on the grounds of the memorial, but the monument itself was locked so I could not see the wall with all the names. The few people walking by did not know why it was locked nor who to contact to get a key to unlock the gate leading to it.

Later I found out that the monument was now kept locked deliberately because on the day of its dedication, with all the TV cameras, dignitaries, Belgian officials, famous survivors, and other distinguished guests who had turned out for the opening ceremonies, the place had been in shambles: beer cans, broken bottles, garbage, and dog feces littered the ground. There were chips in the walls and graffiti sprayed everywhere. Swastikas had been painted with "Sales Juifs" (Dirty Jews) and "Aux Fours" (Back to the ovens) scrawled in several places. Although cleaned up since then, the monument was now kept locked up. Maurice Pioro would get me a key on my next visit to Belgium. Learning about this anti-Semitic incident made me fearful, and I realized that one of my discomforts in Belgium had been that I had felt so Jewish there and once again vulnerable.

Around noon Jeanne's daughter, Martine, and her six-year-old granddaughter, Aurore, came home for lunch. Martine was a thin, chic woman in stylish French clothes, and her daughter, a lively child with big squinting eyes, was very excited at meeting a visitor from America. She shook my hand and burst out in English: "I am happy to meet you," then ran back giggling and blushing to her mother. She had memorized the sentence two days ago and had repeated it over and over so as not to forget it. Small talk flowed easily while we were eating; the food was good and the portions copious.

After the meal, Martine and her daughter went back to school and asked me to go with them. Holding my hand, Aurore talked about her teachers and friends, and then when we reached the school grounds, she introduced me to them as her new friend. The children, all little girls, looked at me shyly, and then one of them said "OK," and another one, "Me," and someone else screamed, "Hamburger." Aurore had already told everyone about the American lady visiting. Then Martine introduced me to her colleagues. "Glad to meet you. We've heard so much about you," they said. Were they referring to my being hidden with Aurore's great-grandparents during the war, or to the fact that I was someone visiting from America? In either case, their attention made me feel uneasy and very much on display. Later in Aurore's class, the children made clear what they were interested in hearing about. Did I watch *Dallas* on TV? Did I know Michael Jackson? Had I been to Disneyland? One little girl said she knew English because her neighbors were American. When I spoke to her in English, she turned very red and would say nothing, bowing her head, but when I left the room, she blurted out, "Bye, bye," and the other children repeated it with much laughter.

Back at the house, Jeanne and I talked while she did the dishes; she would not let me help. Marcel, her husband, puttered in the garden. He used to be an auto mechanic, had worked for the bus company for many years, but had taken early retirement because of a terrible traffic accident, which disabled him for a long time. I didn't find out the nature of the accident. Now he worked in the garden and chopped wood for the enormous stove in the living room that heated the whole floor. There were logs everywhere, in the garden, in the garage, on the porch—neat little stacks. He ran errands for Jeanne; he kept the car spick-and-span; he took care of the dog and the three cats. Jeanne sewed purses at home all day, watched little Nicholas, and made lunch for Aurore, Martine, and Marcel; lunch is the big meal of the day in Belgium. Every July, when the entire country is on vacation, they all went to Spain. They had bought an apartment there not far from the beach that they shared with another family. Everyone loved the water, the cookouts. They seemed such a tight family packed into a neat, orderly, and ordinary life so different from my own. I felt outnumbered and unsettled by comparison. Had there really been a German occupation here forty years ago, or did I dream it?

Jeanne did not talk much about the war, but she did remember some things. She had been very happy at my arrival in 1943, she said. She had two older siblings who were already married and living on their own. "I felt I was getting a little sister," she said, and told me that I had been a very mischievous three-year-old, often getting her into trouble. "We had such good times together," she continued. "Once, when the Germans came to the house, we ran and hid in the fields. It was a game."

"Wasn't I homesick and crying all the time?" I asked.

"Only the first few days," she said. "The first day, after the woman who brought you left, you cried and cried, and I was told that you kept saying, 'My mother is going to come, my mother is going to come.' I didn't understand because you were speaking in a Jewish language."

"I must have been speaking Yiddish."

"Yes. You kept saying that over and over. You wouldn't let us undress you, so my mother put you in bed with your clothes on, with me. Your suitcase stayed on the floor beside the bed because that's where you wanted it. My mother didn't dare open it since you were so upset. The next morning when she did open it, the first thing she saw, right on top of your clothes, was a big, very fine-tooth comb. Too late! We had slept together, and by then I was also covered with head lice."

It was hard to imagine that my mother had let me have head lice. I almost didn't believe that story, but then I remembered the sharp, white powder shampoos Mama Gine had given me and the hours of hair combing. I had thought it was some sort of a game and had submitted to it willingly, although I found it hard to sit still for so long.

I asked if my speaking only Yiddish hadn't been difficult or dangerous for everyone.

"Yes, we didn't let you go out at first. We didn't understand what you wanted or were saying, and you talked a lot once you stopped crying. But you learned Flemish very fast. I was your teacher," she said with pride.

I thought of the language repressed and what it had meant for me. I remember sitting with my mother in a shed, when months later she visited. We spoke in Yiddish then, which my mother was afraid I would forget; she made me recite all the names: her name, my father's name, my own secret name, which no one knew here, my uncle Fischel's name, and the address I was to ask to be taken to if anything happened to her and she stopped visiting.

I told Jeanne what Martin had said about the meetings with my mother when she came to Beersel to see me.

"Yes," Jeanne said. "You and your mother met in a tool shed behind my brother's electrical supply store. My brother is much older than I, and he was already married at the time of the war and lived in the main square in an apartment above his store. On the days your mother visited, I brought you to his shop. Then, when your mother came, she went into his store like an ordinary customer, and if there was no one else around, went through the back door, then through the courtyard, and to the tool shed, where you would be waiting. When it was time to go, she simply left through the store again. She always brought you food, which she made you eat right then and there. I don't know why, maybe she thought we didn't feed you enough," Jeanne said, and laughed. "My mother always gave you a meal before your mother's visit; she didn't want you to meet her on an empty stomach. So you understand with all the stuff your mother made you eat in the shed, no wonder you were always sick after she left. It never failed. You would say your stomach hurts, then you would throw up and be sick all night, and you would cry and cry." I thought there had probably been more to my tears than an upset stomach, but I didn't say anything.

Jeanne showed me a picture of her mother before she died about twenty years ago. She looked emaciated, not at all like the Mama Gine I had remembered; cancer had made her skinny, while in my memory she had been quite plump. After her death, Jeanne's father came to live with her and stayed until his own death about three years ago. She showed me his last photo—an old man, ninety-something, cheeks caved in, wrinkled forehead. I quickly turned to a much earlier picture where he is handsome, mustached, with laughing eyes and dimples—that's how I remember him. Why couldn't I have come a few years earlier? He might still have been alive, and I would have seen him. Suddenly, I remembered how much I had loved him, perhaps transferring my feelings for my lost father onto his gentle person, and a wave of sadness hit me at the idea of his death. I had missed my father, whom I hardly remembered after the war, not realizing that the father I missed was perhaps as much, if not more, Papa Franz Walschot. I don't think I realized this during my visit, but I could not account for the grief I suddenly felt at Jeanne's father's death.

"You know," Jeanne said, as though reading my mind, "my father would have been be so happy to see you today. Oh, I wish he were still alive for it. He talked about you all the time after you left. He kept saying, 'I hope nothing happened to our Astrid.' You see, you were *our* Astrid. And when we heard that they were bombing Brussels again where you were living, he would say, 'I hope Astrid is safe. What a shame we don't hear from her.' And my mother! Let me tell you, there wasn't a night she didn't cry, worrying about you, missing you."

I was very touched and remembered how before my visit to her brother, Martin, it never occurred to me that in all those years the Walschots might be thinking about me, wondering if I was all right, what had become of me. They had probably been hurt that I never contacted them. I can't explain why I have no recollection of leaving them, although our parting must have been painful; they had been my family for almost two years. In my memory, I had been so focused on my happiness at being reunited with my mother that I had erased the separation from the Walschots. Perhaps my mother was right; I had been a child and children forget, or had I deliberately erased that separation from my mind?

"You know," I explained, "lately, I thought a lot about you all.

I didn't know how to find you. When I asked her, my mother said she had forgotten the address, even your names. She said it would be impossible to find you."

"Oh, I understand," Jeanne went on. "Those were terrible times. I think your mother just wanted to forget them. Besides, the important thing is that you are here now."

"Why did I leave?" I asked. "Why didn't I stay until the very end of the war?" I told her that although my coming to them in 1943 is my first conscious memory, I had absolutely no recollection of my leaving them when I was five.

"I think you stayed until your mother thought it was safe to take you back. Perhaps sometime after the landing of the Allies in 1944. Your mother came to fetch you then. I remember I went with you to the train station, carrying your little suitcase, the same suitcase you had when you first came to us."

I visited other people with Jeanne and Marcel in Waterloo that evening before they drove me back to Brussels. First their son-in-law, then some old friends. Many cups of coffee, many pieces of cake, many glasses of wine. Everyone seemed so happy to meet me, but not one word was said about the war. I was asked many things about America, about TV, about President Reagan.

Three days later when I was leaving Brussels to go back to Paris, Jeanne called me and offered to drive me rather than my taking the train. She said that she and Marcel wanted to take the opportunity to visit some friends there. I felt I needed some time alone to reflect about our reunion as it had drained me emotionally; it seemed like Jeanne wanted to reclaim her "Astrid." But I wasn't Astrid anymore, and in some ways I had never been; that identity had been a way of hiding, and even though our reunion had brought out feelings of love for her parents, it had also stirred notions of old fears—the secrecy I was sworn to as a child; my guilt and my anguish at not being able to be with my mother, my torn allegiances, my helplessness at all these separations. I didn't want to be reclaimed. I started to refuse their offer, but Marcel got on the phone and told me that Jeanne really had her heart set on it, so I accepted.

We found ourselves caught in a truckers' strike and blockage of the highway on the day we left. What was to have been a three-hour drive from Brussels to Paris turned into a ten-hour journey. By the time we reached the apartment where I was staying, it was one o'clock in the morning. Jeanne thought it too late to come up and meet my French friends, so we said our good-byes in the car. Two weeks later, I called them from the airport on my way back to the United States. I told Jeanne that now that contact had been reestablished, I would keep in touch. It is a promise I kept, for a while.

LA HULPE, 1982

It wasn't difficult to find La Hulpe when Richard and I drove there after leaving Beersel; it turned out to be only eighteen miles from Brussels. The village looked like a well-to-do suburb: freshly painted, small houses with colorful window shutters, neat little gardens full of eager flowers. I hadn't remembered all that prettiness, but it had probably been different forty years ago during the war when it seemed to be worlds away from where my mother lived.

The streets were deserted when we got there, and I was reluctant to start ringing doorbells and interrupt a family Sunday meal with my story. We saw a man watering his lawn and asked him if he knew where we could find L'Oeuvre Royale du Grand Air pour les Petits. Never heard of it. Had he lived here long? Twenty years, what were we looking for? A home for children, homeless children, foundlings, orphans. He didn't know of any but said that there once was a convent on the outskirts of town that took in children, though he didn't think it still existed. Maybe the home we were looking for had moved; maybe it had changed names. He gave us vague directions to the convent that weren't helpful. We thanked him and left.

While we were driving around La Hulpe, suddenly a street felt familiar, and I asked Richard to turn right and drive into it. Then I began to direct him, not knowing beforehand what my next instruction would be but somehow sensing where to go just as I had sensed where the Walschot house was in Beersel. We wound up driving on a private alley shaded by two rows of trees: here, too, an unconscious recognition of surroundings surfaced. It was a very beautiful and quiet spot.

"Yes," I said, excited, "this is it. The grounds of the home were very big and well kept. I remember this alley; it will lead us to a large garden that I always thought of as a park."

We came up to an iron gate. Behind it were lawns, little circles of rosebushes, stone benches, and quiet nooks overlooking grassy slopes.

"This is it, this is it," I yelled as I jumped out of the car.

There was a plaque at the gate that read: LA RETRAITE DES SOEURS DU SÉNACLE (a retirement home for nuns). The white buildings in the distance looked unfamiliar; I knew I had not seen them before. *Dead end*, I thought, with a sinking feeling that we were not going to find anything. We left the retirement home and continued to drive around the empty streets of La Hulpe for a while, until we came up to a man washing his car in the driveway of his house and asked him about the orphanage. No, never heard of it, but he had only lived here for the last few years. Did we mean the convent?

However vague my memories were, I was sure the place I was looking for had not been a convent. A convent would have meant "nuns," and nuns wore habits; those black clothes would have made a big impression on a child, especially a Jewish child for whom those outfits would have seemed exotic. But perhaps the nuns would know something. It hadn't occurred to me that the home would no longer exist. Were there no more homeless children who needed to be taken in?

The best thing to do was to go to city hall and consult the archives. But since it was Sunday, city hall was closed. I didn't think I wanted to change my plans and come back another day; it would have been the sensible thing to do, but I was already too discouraged to think of coming here again. I was beginning to feel that I was on a fool's errand. Was my search really worth all this time and effort?

Thinking that perhaps the orphanage had become a convent after

I left, we drove around looking for it and found it. It was an abandoned white-brick building with bare windows and neglected lawns overgrown with thorny bushes and weeds. The rusty iron gate leading to it was unlocked. We opened it, walked up to the building, knocked at the door, then banged: no answer. The building seemed deserted. We walked around it; more thorny bushes, weeds, and tall, dry grass everywhere. A row of outdoor toilet stalls appeared in the back of the yard behind the building. The memory of being punished by being locked into an outdoor toilet stall for what felt like hours suddenly flooded into my mind. I was barefoot and shivering with cold, afraid that I would never be let out again, that I had been forgotten, abandoned. It had been a standard punishment then for the little girls who misbehaved. Were those the terrible toilets? They looked vaguely familiar, but I could no longer be sure. In retrospect, it seemed such a cruel and sadistic punishment that I wondered if I hadn't imagined it, but suddenly I felt oppressed, and I was having difficulty breathing. I hadn't thought of the orphanage for years, but now I remembered how unhappy I had been there, unhappy and afraid. Afraid, mostly because I thought my mother would never come to retrieve me, that I had done something that made this impossible, although I didn't know what. I just thought that whatever happened was my fault, and I had cried many nights over my imagined wrongdoing; now I was experiencing a feeling of guilt, although I didn't know if the guilt was about past misbehavior, or about misjudging my mother's motives, or about having forgotten La Hulpe.

With its small windows, its stern facades, and its isolation, the building looked like a prison. Richard and I peeped in through the windows and saw empty rooms, stacks of plaster debris on the floor against the walls, peeling ceilings, every now and then a blackboard; there had been a school here once. All the doors of the building were locked. A few of the windowpanes had been broken, but, by and large, vandals had spared the building.

When I told him I wanted to take a look, Richard picked up one of the bricks lying on the ground and threw it at a window in the basement floor. Then, putting his hand carefully through the broken glass, he unlocked the latch and pulled the window up to open it. I was a little shocked at his action and reluctant to trespass, but with his encouragement, I followed him and climbed into the basement. From there, we walked through a series of empty rooms that held every now and then a broken chair, a few iron cots, and in one room a row of yellowing sinks. Another room was long and narrow. Could that have been a dormitory?

The place had the sad, stark look of impersonal institutions, but my own mood changed: instead of feeling sad at the misery I thought I had felt here, I was overcome by a sudden rage. I found myself running from room to room, kicking the walls, and banging my hands against them, yelling, "I hate you, I hate you!" I was a five-year-old again, venting her helplessness and frustration in a temper tantrum. This kick was for the counselors who had been mean to me, that blow was for the little girls who had hit me and called me names, but mostly this hitting was for everyone who had abandoned me: the Walschots, who must have turned me out; my father, who promised to be right back and wasn't; and mostly my mother, who wouldn't take me home now when she came to visit. Richard stood back and watched me, and did not try to soothe me. After a while I calmed down, embarrassed but mostly surprised at my behavior. Was I losing control over turbulent emotions I did not even know I had?

"I don't know if it was the place," I told Richard. I wasn't sure anymore; I didn't feel the spark of the recognition I had felt in Beersel, when I had recognized the Walschots' house.

"Let's get out of here," I said. We walked down what appeared to be the main staircase and landed in a rather elegant hallway: chandeliers, marble columns, and dozens of cartons filled with old clothes, broken toys, and used utensils lay on the floor. The boxes seemed full of old stuff people dump on their lawns, hoping to sell it to passing motorists.

After leaving the building, we drove down the street and asked a woman who was unlocking her front door if she knew anything about the convent. She told us that the convent had been closed a few years ago for lack of funds, but that some of the Sisters who had run it still lived together in town, in fact, right across the street from the convent. Was the convent there during the war? She didn't know, she wasn't from here, but why didn't we ask the Sisters? They were bound to be home; they never went anywhere. Declining her offer to come in for a cup of coffee, we thanked her and drove back to the convent, then walked up to the house across from it.

The nun who answered the door, Sister Marie Gabrielle, was elderly, plump with a chubby, round face and a big smile. I explained why we were here.

"Please come in," she said, and showed us to a small living room, with a sofa, easy chairs, some magazines. She had one leg shorter than the other, which gave her a jerky, limping walk.

"Yes, the convent did exist during the war," she said, "but I don't know if there were Jewish children hidden there. I myself was not there then, and neither were any of the other Sisters living in the house today. But there are records. Sister Thérèse takes care of them. She went out for a while but should be back in thirty minutes." Why didn't we wait? While we waited, Sister Marie Gabrielle showed me a booklet.

"This is what the convent used to look like," she said. It had been called Malaise, ("Discomfort," what a strange name for a convent, but that was the name of one of La Hulpe's hamlets) and had been a boarding school run by the Sisters of the Sacred Heart. The booklet was a series of sepia photographs turned into postcards; there was one with a view of the garden, another of a parlor, one of a dormitory, another still of a series of alcoves, one of a room with long wooden tables with benches and white bowls, others of classrooms, and so on. I remember going to school at La Hulpe; I had learned some French there, and when I eventually came back to live with my mother, I entered public school in the middle of the third grade and was able to catch up with my schoolmates. Now those photos looked familiar and strange at the same time. I began to doubt and mistrust my own memories and intuitions. I had no doubt that the institution I had stayed at in La Hulpe had not been a convent—and yet? If this had been the place, why didn't I feel sparks of recognition? Should I just give up my search? I felt unsure of myself.

"Would you like to take the book to America?" Sister Marie Gabrielle asked.

I said I would. "But you have to return it to me eventually," she continued, "because it is the only one I have. You'll have to bring it back in person. But you will probably forget all about Sister Marie Gabrielle when you go to America."

I assured her that I would not. I was taken aback by her remark, which struck me as somewhat personal for such a short acquaintance. Later I thought that she had probably been thinking of her former students who had not kept in touch after they graduated. I confess I never did go back and still have the booklet she lent me. She asked us to come into the kitchen for a cup of coffee while she went to find out what was keeping Sister Thérèse, the keeper of the record. This time we did not refuse.

"She'll be here in twenty minutes," Sister Marie Gabrielle said after her phone call. "Perhaps in the meanwhile you would like a tour of the convent? It might jog mademoiselle's memory."

We couldn't tell her that mademoiselle had already been inside the convent by breaking a window, so we sheepishly accepted her offer and went with her across the street into the building again, but this time through the front door.

I really hated being there again, feeling uneasy because we were deceiving her in pretending to look at everything for the first time. Because of her limp, our walking was rather slow. I told her I didn't have to see all the rooms, then asked about the cartons full of old clothes. She explained that they were having a rummage sale the next day to raise funds for one of their charitable institutions. The people of La Hulpe had come by during the week to drop off things.

When we crossed the street again, Sister Thérèse was back. She went into her office and came out with a stack of books. She looked up my name in 1944, 1945, and 1946; it wasn't there. She tried the name I had in hiding, Astrid Von der Laar—still no luck; then my real name at the time, Astrid Katz: it wasn't there either.

"You know," she said, "there is another institution for children in town. It is called Institut de la Reine Astrid, in memory of the Swedish queen of Belgium who was so popular. I don't know if it existed during the war, but since your home was called L'Oeuvre Royale, it means it was probably sponsored by the royal family. I know the director of the place. Why don't I call her to see if she has any information for you? Perhaps there are records."

Perhaps. Hope sprang again. Sister Thérèse went out to call and came back.

"The director wasn't there during the war, but there are records. The place is closed because the children have been taken somewhere on vacation, but she will meet you there right now, if you like, and look at the records for you."

Sister Marie Gabrielle said she would come with us to show us the way and introduce us: we thanked Sister Thérèse and left. Sister Marie Gabrielle seemed to enjoy the ride in such a fancy car, and she was especially impressed by the telephone between the two front seats. "Just imagine," she kept saying.

The Institut de la Reine was very different from the convent: a small, bright building, with flowers on the window boxes; I was sure I had never seen it before. Could it have changed that much? The director, waiting for us by the front door, was a young, fashionably dressed woman with a stylish hairdo.

I apologized for disrupting her Sunday afternoon, but she assured me that it was no trouble as she lived very close by and she wanted to help. She led us indoors to a small office. She had no idea if the institute had hidden Jewish children during the war, but there were records, and we could look to see if my name was in them. She went to a file cabinet and took out several leather-bound notebooks.

No Astrid Von der Laar, no Astrid Katz in them. I had been pretty sure they wouldn't be there because nothing looked the slightest bit familiar; the director was sorry that she couldn't help us. The best thing was to go to city hall in the morning; perhaps they had records. We thanked her and left.

Sister Marie Gabrielle looked as disappointed as I was. We drove her home.

"Don't forget Sister Marie Gabrielle," she said as she got out of the car. "I will pray that you find what you are looking for," she added, then went up the stairs to her house.

Well, we had run into dead ends; I had not been in the convent as a child, nor had I been in the Institut de la Reine Astrid. I was ready to throw in the towel, but Richard suggested that we give the Retreat for Nuns another shot since I had been so sure that it was the place I was looking for. I reluctantly agreed, and we went back to it.

As we drove into the alley again, I had the same sense of recognition. I couldn't understand why I kept seeing images of children in pinafores, interposed on the lush greenery. This time we parked and walked toward the main building. There were women around, elderly women, sometimes in pairs, but mostly alone, sitting on benches or strolling in the alleys, book in hand. None of them wore a habit, but the place had a religious hush about it, a feeling of peace and serenity—very different from what I had remembered. We found the director of the Retreat.

No, she didn't know the home I was looking for, but, of course, she hadn't been here during the war—after all that had been forty years ago. She was sure the Retreat for Nuns wasn't that old, but there was a nun here who had lived in the village in the 1940s. She might be able to help us. She was resting in her room, but perhaps she was up to seeing me. She would go and find out. Why don't we wait?

We looked around a bit while she was gone. Such calm and gentleness: women smiling kindly as they walked by. The buildings were beautiful white brick with red veins. As we peeked in the dining room, we saw white tablecloths, flowers and plants everywhere. I felt totally disoriented, and yet . . .

The director came back with another woman. She looked about eighty years old, very alert. Could she help us? I asked my questions.

"No, this hadn't always been a retreat for nuns," she said. It had been made into one about twenty years ago. She wasn't sure what had been there during the war, but in any case, it had not been a religious institution. She seemed to think that it had been a home for children.

"L'Oeuvre Royale du Grand Air pour les Petits?" I asked.

Sounded familiar, she thought. She didn't remember the name, but she thought it had been such an institution.

Bingo! My instincts had been right after all.

"Of course, you could check the records in city hall," she added, "but that name sounds right."

When I asked if those were the original buildings, she told me that when the Order had bought the property, they had demolished the buildings, which were run-down, and had built the white houses. No wonder I hadn't recognized those big picture windows, those terraces and paved walks—but it was the place, all right!

Strange, I thought that even though the grounds of the Retreat had triggered recognition, when I thought now of the orphanage as we walked around, I didn't remember anything about the other children who were there also, all little girls; I think I was the youngest. Years after I was reunited permanently with my mother, I was surprised to find two photographs of La Hulpe in one of her albums. I don't know why they were taken or what the occasion was, but both photos showed two adult women who were the counselors, and a dozen little girls lined up, and I am the smallest one by far. We all wore gray pinafore aprons that were our uniforms. I don't remember my arrival there, but I remember having my hair cut immediately, very short, with straight bangs across my forehead; it was easier to keep it free of lice that way. Gone were my long curls that had been my mother's joy to comb; even Mama Gine used to like brushing my hair, and Jeanne was always putting bows in it. Here, we all had the same haircut, the same clothes, the same shoes. I remember having to line up all the time, to go outside, to go inside, to go to church, to go to class, to go to eat, and to go to sleep.

The dining room had long wooden benches and tables with lines of bowls set on them; we ate porridge three times a day. On Sundays, as a big treat, we each had an egg and a piece of fruit. We were always monitored. I remembered I was always cold. The stone floors had no rugs; the bathrooms were icy; the toilets were outdoors. The rooms had high ceilings, drafty windows. It seemed that everything could only be reached through long, dark, damp corridors.

For a while the director—whom I remember as a tall, dark, heavy, handsome woman—seemed to take a particular liking to me. She would often single me out to talk to, asking how I was doing. Every now and then, she would send for me and have me eat dinner with her. I don't remember what was served, but for me it was wonderful to be alone with someone, to have a private moment, not to have to share something with forty or so other little girls; I was five and a half by then.

She started to have me sleep with her. I remember a soft bed, a red eiderdown coverlet, and big pillows. She wore a white nightgown; her long black hair hung down her back in a single braid. And she would comfort me, telling me what a sweet child I was. But something happened one evening; I displeased her. I don't really remember how or what I did, but I remember that I wound up crying in her bed. She was very put out and brought me back to the dormitory. After that incident, she hardly spoke to me again. Later she told my mother that I was a very difficult child who always demanded special concessions and who had a violent temper. It wasn't until now when that memory flooded my mind that I realized the woman was a pedophile. Did she want to touch me or have me touch her, and I refused and cried? I don't remember the details of that evening except that I didn't want to do something and she got angry. It was probably just as well, since she left me alone after that incident, but I missed the warmth of her affection and the pride of being singled out.

I caught every childhood disease there, including pneumonia and jaundice. That meant long periods of isolation in a room with periodic visits from a nurse. My illnesses aggravated my sense of loneliness and abandonment; I often felt I would be forgotten in the sickroom, that no one would come to rescue me.

After a while my mother came to see me regularly. By then the war was over, and there was no longer any danger of her being arrested and disappearing. Yet each time she was due, I awaited her visit with trepidation, afraid that she wouldn't show up, that something terrible had happened to her. Remembering this today, I am a little confused, but I know that I was no longer in hiding at the time. The records in Brussels showed that I had been placed in the orphanage on January 16, 1945. Jews were no longer in danger by then, but I didn't know why I was there, nor do I know it now except that my mother had told me that she couldn't take me yet; I had to be patient.

Meanwhile, we would often spend Sunday afternoons together. As she had done in Beersel, my mother brought me presents, mostly food: oranges, apples, chocolate. We would go on a picnic on the grounds and eat it all.

Sometimes she brought a friend with her, Hélène, a woman I got to know and love later, but mostly she came with a man called Landau. He brought me toys. He wanted to marry her, my mother told me later. He was very sweet to me, but I distrusted him; was he keeping my mother from taking me back? Landau kept up his court-ship once my mother and I were reunited, and he continued to pay much attention to me. Eventually, I learned to trust him and grew so attached to him that when my mother broke up with him and he disappeared from our lives, I missed him, even after my mother told me that the reason she stopped seeing him was that he didn't want to be saddled with a child. It is only now in writing about these years that I realized that this was the same David Landau who had courted her in Antwerp before my mother married my father. Landau had survived the war and resumed some kind of amorous relationship with her.

Landau turned out to be one of a string of boyfriends my mother had after the war; none of them lasted. Each time they vanished, my mother would tell me that she had ended the relationship because of me, that these men wanted to send me to boarding school. Later on, when I was grown up, she told me that the reason that she broke up with them was that she didn't want to tell them that she wore a wig. I don't remember my mother mentioning that when I was a child; for me, perhaps because I was used to seeing her without her wig, I never thought it strange or abnormal that she had no hair. I would not have understood how her baldness could be the reason for the disappearance of these men.

On one of her visits, my mother brought a very thin young man, who upon seeing me burst into tears and hugged me, and kept on kissing me. He seemed very upset that I did not remember him. He was my father's youngest brother, Benjamin, who had played the role of go-between during my parents' courtship before the war; he would eventually settle in Israel. He had been deported from Antwerp at the age of seventeen and had survived Auschwitz to come back to Belgium. At that time, in the summer of 1945, no one knew what had happened to my father after he was deported. My uncle was going to go back to Germany to look for him. He would find him, he told us, not to worry: he never did find him but ran into some Israelis who talked him into smuggling himself into Israel to join the fight for its independence. I didn't care anymore if he found my father or not. I just wanted my mother to take me home with her. Why couldn't I go home? I spent most of my mother's visits crying and asking to go home. I told her things were terrible at the orphanage. I lied; I exaggerated; I made up stories. I told her they were beating me, which was not true.

My mother took me by the hand and went to the director of the orphanage and told her my accusations; she in turn called in the counselors, who denied my allegations. I broke down and cried and admitted that they weren't true and promised not to tell lies again. Everyone forgave me, but everyone seemed to keep their distance afterward; I was a troublemaker.

My mother told me that if I didn't behave better during her visits and stop asking to go home, she would stop coming. That brought on more tears, and I promised to be a good girl, never to lie again. But when she was leaving, I clung to her crying, wanting to go home. At times I think I hated her for abandoning me. I was sure she was having a secret life somewhere without me.

Earlier I had lived with another kind of fear, that of her being taken by the Germans. The end of the war on May 8, 1945, five months after I was placed in the orphanage, didn't mean much to me; I was too young to understand the significance of the armistice, and, besides, nothing had changed for me; I was still here, separated from my mother.

I used to stand by the gate on the days of her visits and wait for her. Once, when she didn't come, I sobbed all afternoon by the gate, convinced that she had been arrested. I could not be made to understand that there was no such danger anymore. After all, every separation, every loss, every upheaval that had happened in my life until then was due to someone being caught by the Germans and being taken away.

I lived for my mother's visits and with the fear that she might not come, that something had happened to her. Later on I lived with the fear that she wouldn't come because she didn't love me anymore. I knew I was a bad child, having been told that so often in La Hulpe, and in my heart of hearts, I knew that everything bad that had happened was my fault, even if I didn't quite understand what I had done. That was why Mama Gine and Papa Franz didn't want me anymore, and why I had had to leave their family in Beersel. The reason why my father had disappeared was because I had done something terrible, and now I was afraid that my mother might not love me anymore.

That fear did not vanish once my mother and I were reunited and lived together again. I was almost eight then. As excited to go home as I must have been, I don't remember my last day at the orphanage, just as I don't remember my last day with the Walschots in Beersel—but I do remember the circumstances of our reunion. My mother told me that there was a confusion in La Hulpe about my homecoming; she had changed her mind about the date and had written them to ask that I be kept for a few more weeks, as she wasn't ready for me yet. (She said she had had an operation and wasn't fully recovered; I never found out what kind of operation.) Either La Hulpe didn't get her letter or it came too late because I was put on a train for Brussels by myself on the agreed-upon date. As neither my mother nor any of her neighbors had a telephone, it hadn't occurred to her to call and check.

I panicked when there was no one to greet me at the train station when I arrived in Brussels and, crying, walked around looking for my mother. I thought she had not come on purpose, that she really didn't want me and that La Hulpe had sent me home to get rid of me. Perhaps it had only been a matter of ten minutes of sheer terror of being alone in the station, but to me it seemed like hours spent walking around looking for her.

Then I saw her. She was with her girlfriend Hélène. My mother was wearing a fur coat I vaguely recognized and a smart little hat. I thought she looked beautiful, but when I called out to her, she looked right through me. It was her friend who saw me first. "There's Dori," she screamed. My mother ran over and we hugged: we hadn't seen each other for weeks. I had just gotten over the chicken pox, and my face was still covered with sores. Somehow the metal tip of one of my shoelaces had gotten embedded in my ankle and infected it, and I had had to have it surgically removed; I was bandaged and limping. My hair had been cut extra short so I would look neat for my mother; my ears stuck out. I had lost a lot of weight, but my stomach was swollen.

My mother had not been expecting me since she had written La Hulpe asking them not to send me home that weekend. But all day long, she had had a premonition. She was with Hélène and kept telling her, "I hope they didn't put her on that train. They must have gotten my letter." What she didn't tell her was that because she was semi-literate, she wasn't sure she had made herself clear. She had always thought her handwriting was illegible, and she was deeply ashamed of it; later, although still a child, I did all her writing for her, but now she didn't even tell her best friend why she thought that her letter had not been understood. Finally, Hélène told her, "If you are so worried, why don't we just go to the train station and see?" And hopping in a cab, they had hurried down, worrying that I was there. My mother had not recognized me at first glance, but I was so happy to see her that at the time I thought I didn't care what had happened. I just hung on to her hand and wouldn't let go.

The first couple of months of our reunion were difficult. In spite of my being happy to be with my mother, I couldn't forget what had happened in the train station when I had come home. Had she really not known that it was me, or had she pretended not to recognize me because she really didn't want me? It was hard for both of us to adjust to each other. My mother worked long hours for a furrier, and she would come home exhausted from the difficult sewing all day. She was still young, in her thirties, and she liked to go out on her one day off rather than being saddled with me. She wasn't used to having to care for a child anymore, and I wasn't an easy child. There had been so many separations in my life, I couldn't get over my fear that something would happen and I would be sent away again. I had to constantly test my mother's love. I ran away from home several times after quarreling with her. Once, I climbed onto the roof of our house and wouldn't come down for a long time. I broke things; I hit other children in temper tantrums. In La Hulpe, to get along with the other little girls and to win the approval of the counselors, I had held so many feelings bottled up inside me, it felt good to release them, even though they were aimed at inappropriate targets.

I didn't miss my father anymore because I no longer remembered him. When I thought of him, I sometimes pictured him alive somewhere with a different family, and I would feel great pain, or I would be very angry and hope that he was really dead. My mother tried to reason with me when I misbehaved. She told me that I was not like the other children; I had no father, which, in those days, was not a common situation. All my friends and schoolmates had two parents; as a single-parent family, we did stick out in our little world in Brussels. I had to understand, she said, how difficult it was for her, how hard she worked. I had to help by being good and listening to her; she couldn't do everything around the house herself. I would have to be more responsible: If I didn't behave, she would have no choice but to send me away to some boarding school. I didn't know if she meant it, but the threat scared me; that was the worst thing that could happen—it meant La Hulpe all over again.

I promised I would behave, but mostly I went on with my stunts anyway. We argued all the time; I was as stubborn as she was. I had been brought up by a Catholic family in a small Flemish town and by a mixture of kind and indifferent strangers in an institution. I had manners that puzzled her as I had been taught to do things differently from the way she did them: I didn't like her cooking and wanted to eat things she had never heard of. I wanted the toys my classmates had, but my mother couldn't afford them. She was impatient with me when I talked about people she didn't know. I loved being without all the other children of the institution, but I felt constrained and threatened with the responsibilities of intimacy that she imposed on us, and I clung to some of the rituals I had been performing before I came home. When my mother caught me saying grace before meals, crossing myself in front of a church, or praying to Jesus at night, she became very upset. For a while, we were like strangers to each other.

Then there was the question of languages. I hadn't forgotten Yiddish, my first language, but I didn't want to speak it anymore. I felt it identified us as Jews, and I was ashamed when my mother spoke it to me in public; I would pretend not to understand, and I would always answer in French, which she, in turn, did not know well. Looking back, I don't know whether I was so much ashamed as afraid. Being Jewish meant all sorts of bad things would happen to you. I was too young to realize how the anti-Semitism permeating Belgium affected me, but I knew people looked down on you for being Jewish, and I would always be afraid that if friends in school found out I was Jewish, it would change our relationship. I often lied about it to my little classmates, saying that my mother was Jewish but I wasn't: I swore I believed in Christ.

Of course, to the outside world—meaning school and our neighborhood in Brussels on chaussée d'Etterbeek—I was Astrid, which was my legal name, not Dori. We lived on a street of family-owned small stores: bakeries, butcher shops, notion stores, hardware, et cetera. Children played on the sidewalks as no one had gardens—that is, backyards—in these modest surroundings. Because my mother worked late hours, I often played by myself into the early evening after the other children had gone indoors. All the merchants knew me and were friendly, greeting me as Astrid. Although I did not feel the dichotomy between the two personas of Astrid/Dori that I had felt in hiding with the Walschots, I still sometimes felt like two little girls.

By now, more and more, I thought of myself as Astrid, which my mother never called me. At times this made me doubt her love, since Astrid was who I had become in order to survive and to interact with the outside world—the world where I wanted to belong, blend in. Dori was the little Jewish girl my mother wanted to pull back into her own circumscribed life, which was stifling and dangerous. Besides, I wanted to put the past behind me because I was very much ashamed of all that had happened—my father's disappearance, my being in hiding, then in the orphanage—these were the secrets that I never told anyone. I still clung to the feeling that my family and I had done something awful to deserve what had happened to us, although I didn't know what it was but felt that others did. Although I was no longer in hiding, I was still afraid that I would be found out. I made up stories for my classmates to explain the disappearance of my father: He had been a captain in the Belgian army; he died a brave hero's death fighting the Germans.

I wanted to be invisible—that is to say, like everybody else—which was another reason I wanted to speak only French. I went to a French school; in this bilingual country, my friends were French speaking. They shared their parents' prejudice in thinking that the Flemish people were inferior. Besides not being Jewish, I also did not want to be considered Flemish, even though I was born in the Flemish town of Antwerp. My mother spoke Flemish like a native, which had served her well during the war. With her false papers and false identity, she had easily passed for a Catholic Belgian thanks in part to a lack of accent that would have given her away as a foreigner. Now Flemish was the language she spoke with non-Jews. I also spoke it well; I had learned it in Beersel with the Walschots. Here in Brussels, we had Flemish classes in school twice a week. I made mistakes on purpose, pretended not to know answers, mispronounced words deliberately then laughed.

Many of these issues vanished when we came to the States in 1952. Because World War II did not cast a shadow over my world here, there was no longer a reason to hide. The separation between inner and outer world became fluid. Little by little, I had everyone call me Dori, which my friends assumed was a nickname I had adopted, as they themselves often had nicknames. Citing the reason that we needed to become "American" now, I insisted that my mother and I speak English all the time—a language that, unlike French, she learned pretty well. I mastered it quickly enough to lose my accent within a year so that I was no longer asked where I was from. Mostly I felt invisible, which gave me a sense of freedom. By the time I became an American citizen at the age of eighteen, I had gotten rid of Astrid and legally changed my name to Dori on my naturalization papers.

After I left La Hulpe, I adjusted well in school in Brussels. I was bright and had no trouble catching up with the rest of the third graders. Within a few months, I was at the head of the class, never first but always second or third. I had conflicting emotions about schoolwork. On the one hand, I loved it and did very well. On the other hand, I didn't want to call attention to myself, so I held back, did less well than I could have on purpose. Yet I was proud, and even though I didn't want to be different from my classmates, I needed to be distinguished, "special": I felt that by being special I would earn the right to be here with everyone else. I enjoyed the approbation of teachers. So I alternated between shining in class and failing at some very easy tests.

For a while I think I was one of the few Jewish children in my school in Brussels and was often pointed out as that by the principal and teachers, some of whom knew my history. That kind of attention mortified me. I had good and bad luck with teachers—a few were kind and supportive; others taunted me. I remember one in particular in the fifth grade who would often call on me and ask: "Does the little Jewish girl know the answer?" When she was angry at the class, she would say before recess: "No one will go out to play until the Jewish girl stops fidgeting." She rarely called me by my name.

The other children's responses were mixed. At times they also mocked me, but I think more to please the teacher than from ill feelings toward me. Other times the children consoled me after class, saying the teacher was a witch.

I had good friends to play with, but sometimes we fought, as all children do, and eventually if the fight was passionate enough, I would be called "*sale juif*" (dirty Jew). Rather than angering me, the remark made me feel great fear. I could never respond by yelling "*sale catholique*" but screamed instead that I was *not* Jewish, that it wasn't true.

Walking on the grounds of La Retraite des Soeurs du Sénacle with Richard, I thought that it might have been as peaceful and beautiful in the days I lived here as it was now, and that all the chaos had been in me, in the feelings of fear, abandonment, and anger that the circumstances had engendered. But the place seemed closed to me now, unwilling to take me in. After the anger and depression I had felt all day, a kind of weariness settled in; the place didn't mean anything anymore.

"Let's go," I said to Richard, and we drove back to Brussels and called Martin Walschot.

SAN FRANCISCO, 1985

"Come for lunch at twelve," Arnold had said. As he hadn't moved since the last time I saw him over twenty years ago, I easily found his house on a typically hilly street of San Francisco. He and his new wife must have been watching for me out of their windows because by the time I parked, got out of the car, and climbed the steps to their front door, they were waiting outside. Arnold looked good, still slim, with deep brown eyes, but he was now bald; later he told me he had had a heart attack a year ago and that he would soon be eighty-three.

He introduced me to Louise, his new wife, who embraced and kissed me on both cheeks, and we went to sit in his living room, which smelled of starch; the curtains were just as stiff as when Helen, his second wife, had been alive and washed and ironed them weekly. I had been surprised by his willingness to see me after so many years of not being in touch, but he seemed to bear me no grudge for not contacting him. "*Moyd,*" he said, holding my hand and calling me by the Yiddish word for "maiden"—a nickname he had given me when we first met in Brussels. "*Moyd,* I see Moishe before me," adding that I had my father's eyes, his chin, his smile . . . I was a little taken aback by his bringing my father up so quickly.

———

Arnold and my father had met in Auschwitz; they were housed in the same barracks, and they had shared their life stories. My father told him of his arrest in Brussels, that he was married and had a little three-year-old girl, me. Arnold told him that he had been deported from Poland. Later he learned from other prisoners that his wife and two sons had also been deported to Auschwitz but had been killed as soon as they got off the train; there was no camp numbers for them. Since numbers served as identification, those destined to die right away were not tattooed on the arms. Arnold and my father became friends in the camp, if the notion of friendship still pertained under the circumstances that bound them together. Perhaps anticipating that their chances of surviving were slim, they promised each other that if one of them did survive, he would look out for the other's family; Arnold survived and, having no reasons to go back to Poland, came to Brussels to find out if my mother and I were still alive, keeping his promise to a dead man. He found my mother; I was in the La Hulpe orphanage at the time. After staying in Brussels for a while, he started a business that took him to Germany, where he settled down for a year and remarried.

By the time he came back to live in Brussels with Helen, his new wife, I had left the orphanage at La Hulpe and was home; my mother and I saw them on a regular basis. I must have been about eight years old then. I fell in love with Helen, who opened a new world for me, introducing me to poetry, literature, and music. There were no books in my house, but Helen bought some for me, and read and praised my childish writing when I tried my hand at poetry. I don't know how Helen survived the war in Germany; she did not volunteer her story, and we didn't talk about such things. I did realize that she was very well read and educated. Looking now at the one photograph I have of her, I see that she was plump and rather plain, but I remember a certain grace and elegance in her kindness. The name Helen seems to have played a big role in my mother's and my life. Just as Henna (a version of the name) Wunderman had been so helpful to my mother before and during the war, so did I also think of Helen Golde, Arnold's wife, as a sort of mother. I would often go to their house after school, pulling the tongue of the lion-headed doorbell of their front door with special eagerness. Arnold was seldom home then, off somewhere running business errands, but Helen was always there typing letters, paying bills, translating forms from German into French; she would drop whatever she was doing to give me something to eat and would let me talk about my day at school, my friends, my little problems. My mother worked long hours and was not home when I got back from school; and at night she was too tired to listen to my childish prattle.

When Arnold and Helen left for America, I was devastated, but they promised to bring us over also, and that is how we happened to land in San Francisco in 1952, when I was twelve and a half. We were sponsored by Arnold, who had made all the arrangements for us to get the appropriate visas and residence permits; that also meant signing affidavits saying that he would be financially responsible for us once we arrived. Many papers had to be filled out on both sides of the Atlantic, and my mother and I spent hours in immigration offices in Brussels, answering questions about our motives for leaving, providing certificates of health, explaining our relationship to Arnold—the process took several years.

I am not sure why my mother wanted to come to America. But there were no relatives left in Belgium; Benjamin, my father's youngest brother who had somehow miraculously survived Auschwitz, had gone to Israel; many of my mother's friends had also left for America. Henna Wunderman had died in a botched-up operation in 1950. Arnold convinced my mother that life would be easier and better for us in California. This time, unlike her illegal arrival in Belgium from Poland in the 1930s, she would start a life in a new place with all the required papers; no need for smuggling or hiding.

What I knew of America I had gleaned from the movies I was crazy about. I am not sure that I understood what immigrating meant, but I anticipated no regrets at leaving my friends and my familiar surroundings; I was sure that once we crossed the ocean, I would become a movie star, that it was all preordained. Because the process took so long, it became a sort of dream. On the one hand, the anticipation of leaving held great promise, while, on the other hand, it made life in Brussels seem so impermanent; I think I committed less strongly to my little friends and my schoolwork knowing that soon I would be leaving it all.

In San Francisco, Arnold and Helen ran a boardinghouse near Buena Vista Park that provided breakfast and dinner to their guests. Arnold assumed that once we came, we would live with them and my mother would help by cleaning rooms and cooking at night, but my mother felt insulted by the assumption, accusing Arnold of bringing us over so he could have a maid. Perhaps it reminded her of her situation at her brother Fischel's house in Antwerp when she first arrived from Poland and felt like her sister-in-law's servant. Arnold told her she was being ungrateful, after all the strings he had pulled for us, the lawyers he had hired so that we could emigrate. They quarreled, and a few weeks later we found an apartment and moved out. Thanks to a Jewish agency that helped refugees find work, my mother got a job sewing skirts in a factory.

She cut off all communication with Arnold, but I kept in touch with Helen, often stopping by to visit after school as I had done in Brussels. My mother wasn't happy about this; she felt that out of loyalty I should have shunned them both, but I had no quarrel with them. I didn't share my mother's complaints, didn't see our position in Arnold's household as servile, and in truth I had loved living in the boardinghouse the short while we were there; I had been given a lot of attention by the boarders, who took me out now and then and bought me small presents.

Six months after leaving Arnold's boardinghouse, we left San Francisco for Los Angeles. We had gone there to visit my mother's cousin Henna Wunderman's daughter, Bella, who had been hidden in a convent during the war. My mother preferred Los Angeles, finding it cheaper to live and jobs more plentiful there. Perhaps she also wanted to put more distance between herself and Arnold. I kept up a correspondence with Helen, and years later I would stop in San Francisco to visit on my way home from graduate school when

I was studying for my PhD at the University of Iowa. My mother disapproved of those visits, but she knew I would make them in spite of her objections so she didn't voice them; she just said that she couldn't understand why I would take the time to go out of my way to see people I had so little contact with, especially since my vacations were so short.

Those were delightful visits for me. Helen and I talked and talked, now on a more equal level, since I was no longer a child, about books and music. Arnold was always pleasant to me on those occasions, picking me up at the airport, giving me tours of San Francisco, asking for news about my mother. He had gotten very rich from buying and selling properties in the lucrative San Francisco real estate market. You would not have known this, however, by their modest living style, and Helen told me that Arnold was very tight with his money; instead of bringing him joy, money had become a source of worry and aggravation. He was fearful of losing it, of people taking advantage of him, of passing up promising investments. Helen had very little to do with their finances.

As time went by, I became less attentive and wrote only sporadically, being wrapped up in my own life in Iowa. It was quite a shock when my mother called me one day to tell me she had heard from Arnold several months ago that Helen had been run over by a car and died. My mother said that she hadn't told me earlier because I was away and she didn't want to upset me. Why she thought I would be less upset finding out so much later about Helen's death was a mystery to me; now I had missed the funeral and a chance to say good-bye. I don't know why I didn't contact Arnold then to offer my condolences; maybe I was too embarrassed to express my sympathy and grief, so many months after his wife's death, or perhaps I felt guilty for not having written in so long, or perhaps I was angry at him because the last time I had seen Helen, as she and I were puttering in her garden, she had told me she had been so unhappy with Arnold that she had left him for a couple of months.

In my youthful arrogance, I couldn't understand why a sixty-year-old woman would bother to try to build a new life at her age, but I sympathized with her frustrations at Arnold's dark moods and at his quarrels with their friends, acquaintances, and neighbors, as she told me of her unhappiness. I hadn't realized how difficult living with Arnold had been since he had always been very pleasant to me, and I had dismissed my mother's disparaging remarks about his stinginess and selfishness as part of her grudge against him. But Helen's revelations were not easy to ignore: they made me see Arnold in a different way, not simply as the good-natured and smiling host he had been playing. Maybe my mother hadn't been totally wrong?

Helen told me that Arnold had found out what hotel she was staying at, and he came by every night weeping and begging her to return, which she eventually did. I couldn't help wondering if she would still be alive if she hadn't gone back to him. Had she been so despondent that she absentmindedly walked into the path of a car? With Helen gone, I lost touch with Arnold, but years later I learned, through an acquaintance of my mother's who knew him, that he had married for the third time, another German-Jewish woman.

All the time I knew them, neither Helen nor Arnold talked about the war, although he kept telling me that I was the image of my father, and I never brought up the subject myself. But now, after my trip to Belgium when I had read the papers pertaining to my father's arrest and admission to Auschwitz, I became obsessed by the need to know as much as possible about him: how he had died, what kind of person he had been. It wasn't enough to have my mother tell me repeatedly that I was just like him since that was usually said in exasperation; nor did the assurances of a distant cousin who had known him as a little boy telling me that he had loved children and was always in a good mood bring him to life for me. By now, my own memories of my father were so sparse and vague that I could no longer distinguish between what I remembered and what I had been told. Did I really see myself, at the age of three, standing by a kitchen window watching my father wave good-bye to me with both hands? Or was that a picture described by my mother?

I had kept him in a small corner of my mind for forty years, but the pain I had felt in reading that Auschwitz document had been the most emotional connection I had ever had with him since his disappearance, and I thought I could prolong that connection by learning the details of his life in Auschwitz and of his death; perhaps that would resurrect him. The Auschwitz admission form was dated April 1, 1944: There was no trace of him afterward and, of course, no death certificate—he had simply vanished. After the war, my mother and I had gone to a dozen agencies and offices devoted to the repatriation of camp survivors to see if we could find out what had happened to him. We had filled out many forms, had been interviewed by office personnel, had read over lists of names, but to no avail; there was no information about him—it was as though he had never existed.

Afterward, when I remembered Arnold telling my mother and me that he had been with my father until my father disappeared in January 1945, I had all sorts of questions I had never brought up before. I wrote him asking if I could come visit to talk about my father. By then, I was teaching at a small liberal arts college in New England but still came to California on holidays to see my mother. I wasn't sure Arnold would be willing to replay those painful years, so I was surprised when he wrote back (or rather Louise, his wife, wrote back since he did not write English) that I would always be welcome in his home, and that he would be glad to tell me all that he remembered. The next time I traveled to Los Angeles, I detoured to San Francisco to see him.

"How can you remember after so many years?" I asked; it had been almost forty years. "I remember as if it were yesterday," Arnold said, and began talking about the concentration camps. He talked about them with a kind of vitality and enthusiasm that was puzzling. It was as though those terrible years were the most important ones in his life; they were the driving force of his financial ambition, which turned making money into some kind of revenge, but it wasn't always easy to follow what he was saying. His memory was sketchy; he would drift off, then start again and sometimes contradict himself. There was also the problem of language: I hadn't remembered Arnold's English being so poor; he often searched for words, blaming his new wife, who sat silently besides him, for his lack of fluency. "It's Louise's fault; we always talk in German," he said. His French was nonexistent, and my Yiddish was too weak for me to converse in it.

He started by telling me that my father was a barracks leader in Buchenwald; everyone loved him because he was so fair to all, so kind. At the word "Buchenwald," my heart dropped. Was this just a slip of the tongue? My father was in Auschwitz, not Buchenwald. I told Arnold he was mistaken about the camp, but he shook his head. Then I said that I saw the records in Belgium; it was Auschwitz. "The records lie," he said. I was crestfallen. Could Arnold have been in Buchenwald, and the man he thinks is my father have been someone else? Could it have been another Moishe Katz; was "Katz" such a common name? Then it was not my father he had known? All these years hanging on to the ghost of a memory, to the little intangible portraits of my father that Arnold had given me, my resemblance to him that he sees—and all the time it was someone else? Then what about the years in Belgium with him and Helen, the sponsorship to America? Had it been a mistaken connection?

Arnold asked me the date of the Auschwitz document. "April 1, 1944," I told him. "Oh, that's right, that could be," he said suddenly sheepish, taking my hand again and stroking it. He explained that for a while they were moved from camp to camp, before arriving at Auschwitz, and that he didn't remember all the camp names. This I had read in my father's file: he was arrested in the summer of 1942 but wasn't admitted to Auschwitz until April 1944. There had been a few illegible forms referring to small camps where he had been incarcerated. I had accepted that I would never know what happened to him in those two interim years, but the information tallied with what I had read about the multiplicity of small camps besides the well-known ones. "In Auschwitz," Arnold went on, "it was all so disorderly at the end, especially when the Russians were approaching, and prisoners were being evacuated and forced to walk in the woods in confusion, in *balagan* [disorder]—guards yelling one thing, others yelling something else, go here, go there . . ." Although still shaken, I told myself that Arnold was now confused somewhat in his memories—some slight senility had perhaps set in. Some things he remembered very clearly; others were vague or lost. It had to have been my father he remembered. I can't be absolutely sure that I understood everything he told me, but I pieced his fragmented recollections together into a sort of narrative.

"Your father was a barracks leader," Arnold said.

"Was he chosen by the Germans?" I asked, suddenly afraid I would find out things my father did to survive that would tarnish my image of him.

"Oh, no," said Arnold, "those were the *Kapos*, the brutal criminals they put in charge of us. Your father was barracks leader because everyone loved him, trusted him. He was the one who cut the bread and gave out the portions. That piece of bread was a matter of life and death to us, and his was the most important job. He always gave me the biggest cut, the piece that was left over after all the others were sliced." Here Arnold tried to show me how my father managed to cut the bread so that by a sleight of hand, an extra, unseen slice would remain. He did it over and over, flipping his wrist, but I didn't get it. His wife also tried to explain it, but I'm not sure what she meant. We were all frustrated, Arnold most of all. But the example of the bread was to show that my father protected him, took care of him, gave him extra bread, let him sleep two minutes longer, watched over him in an avuncular way, even though Arnold was older than my father. Arnold had worshipped my father, he told me, and still now his face lit up each time he said, "Your father . . ."

"It wasn't so bad," he continued, "life there. You learned to survive. Your father survived because he had big willpower: you had to be strong, to take it, have willpower. Your father had a lot of willpower. I did too. The worst were the Dutch; they dropped like flies. They had no willpower, they cried, they complained—they did not survive." It seemed so strange to hear him say that life was not horrific there; yet as he talked, his face was animated and his eyes shone in some sort of excitement. Would my father have thought the same thing?

"At the end," he went on, "when the Germans heard that the Russians were coming, we had to leave Auschwitz, and we were forced to march westward, going from place to place, through the woods. The Russians were closing in, or so they said. It was in January, in winter. It was very cold everywhere—you can't believe how cold. Everything was upside down in the camp; soldiers running around giving orders, yelling. After a while we came to a place where there were trains waiting, and they ordered us to board them. I was already on the train, even had a seat, but I noticed that your father wasn't there: I had lost sight of him the last couple of days and now couldn't find him. Against the advice of everyone, I went back looking for him. I looked and looked.

"After a while I found him; he was lying on the ground. I saw that something was wrong with him, with his leg. He could barely walk. I picked him up and carried him on my back," Arnold went on. "I loved him; I carried him to the train. 'Help me,' I asked everyone. 'I have a wounded man here—help me get him on the train.' But no one would help; they were all running, trying to get on the train, trying to get a seat. Finally we got on; the train started, but after a while it stopped. The Germans yelled at us to get off. The railroad tracks had been bombed; we'd have to walk, take another train later. It was very cold." Arnold stopped talking for a while and seemed lost in reverie, his eyes tearing up, then he continued; I was holding my breath.

"I picked up your father, who was too weak to stand on his own, and put him on my back and got off the train. A German guard came over asked me what I was doing. I told him your father couldn't walk and was weak. 'Put him down over there,' he said, indicating a spot on the ground near the tracks, 'and since you are so strong, see those three other Jews over there in the train?' I saw three men lying down in the train corridor, not moving. I didn't know if they were asleep, or dead, or what. They looked very sick. 'Carry those men over there also,' said the guard. I did. I climbed back into the train, and I lifted the men, one by one, put them on my back, and carried them down the train to where your father was lying.

"When all three were there lying on the ground next to your father, the German took out his pistol and shot them, one by one. When he pointed the gun at your father's head, I stopped him. 'Don't shoot him,' I said. 'I'll take care of him, I'll carry him on my back, I can do it. I'm strong. Please, don't shoot him.' The guard hesitated, looked at me and at your father, whose eyes were closed, then shrugged his shoulders, put his gun back in its holster, and walked off.

"I made your father's life longer by maybe a few hours, or a few days, or maybe a week. I don't know. I carried him for a while, then put him down on the ground again and left him to go find out what was happening. A train was coming; we were told to board it. I went back to get your father, but he wasn't there anymore. I asked everyone: 'Where's Moishe Chaim? Have you seen Katz? A redheaded man, bad leg, he was just here.' No one knew. I tried all over. I asked and asked, but no one knew. Finally, I had to get on the train by myself and it left."

Arnold stopped talking for a while, perhaps seeing himself again on that train. I didn't dare interrupt his silence, but I kept asking myself, *Where was my father? Where did he disappear to?* There had to be an explanation.

Suddenly Arnold asked me: "Are you religious?" Not waiting for my answer, he went on, "I am alive today because of your father. Well, in shul the rabbi last Saturday told the story of a man going back to get a friend who was wounded in a battle. Everyone said, 'Don't go. You'll get killed! Are you crazy?' The commander of the unit wouldn't let him go at first, but the man begs and begs, so finally the commander lets him go. When his friend, who is lying on the ground, sees him coming, he says, 'I knew you would come back for me. I knew you wouldn't let me die. You're my friend.' The man lifts his friend on his back and carries him to safety. But by the time they get there, the friend is dead.

"'That man,' said the rabbi, 'that man who carried his friend on his back is a holy man.'" I could barely concentrate to follow Arnold's words now, having an image of a corpse lying in the snow, a redheaded corpse—my father? Had that been how he had died, just expired from exhaustion, or had another German soldier come by and shot him and then had the body taken away? I just couldn't connect with that image, and I realized that Arnold also didn't know exactly how and when my father had died. How could he have disappeared? Perhaps Arnold mistook the place he had left him? Perhaps he hadn't searched long enough?

"That story reminded me of your father," Arnold went on. "I don't think that I am a holy man, but I know that I'm alive today, that I survived all those terrible things, because of your father, because I carried him on my back. After I stopped the German from shooting him, and when I was carrying him on my back, your father said to me, 'Arnold, *in mayn sof, wilst die leben.*'" (Arnold couldn't translate the sentence but when I later looked it up in a Yiddish dictionary, I found that *sof* means "end." So *in mayn sof* means "in my end"; *wilst die leben*, "you will live." Perhaps my father said something like "You will live for me, Arnold, you will live in my stead"?) "It's because of what your father said that I survived," Arnold went on. "I'm not a holy man, I'm just a little religious, but I know in my heart that I survived because of your father, because of what I did for your father.

"Anyway," Arnold continued, "I remembered then of the pact I had made with your father, how I had promised that if I lived through this, I would go to Brussels and find you and your mother. That's why I went to Belgium after the war. I had no place to go to. I didn't want to go back to Poland or to stay in Germany. I knew my wife and sons were dead. The Allies and the Red Cross who were taking care of us when we were liberated would send you back to the country you came from. I remembered someone I knew very well in the barracks who was from Belgium; I remembered he was from Brussels. I knew he was dead. So I lied. I told them I was that man. I told them I was from Brussels. I knew they wouldn't catch me because he was dead, and they had no records. I had no place to go. I had no family. My wife and two sons died in camp. Did you know I had had two sons? Two sons, nine and eleven. In Poland. The day they arrested my wife and sons, a neighbor—not Jewish, a Christian woman—came out of her house and said to my wife, 'Give me the young one. I'll take care of him for you. I'll keep him until you get back.'

"My wife didn't want to. She was afraid to be separated from him, to lose him. 'How will I find him afterward?' she asked. 'It'll be too hard, I won't recognize him. Maybe you'll move. Who knows what will happen? It's better for the three of us to stay together.' Well, they were all gassed together in the camp.

"I found out about that Christian neighbor afterward. After the war, someone told me the story. Maybe my wife told someone on the train to Auschwitz who told me.

"I would have had at least one son." (Arnold started to cry, very quietly. His wife put her hand on his shoulder and squeezed it. After a while he stopped crying and continued.)

"I thought of going back to Poland after the war, for that neighbor, to try to find her. But I had promised your father I would go to Belgium. I had no place to go really.

"So I went to Brussels; I went to Place Rouppe. All the survivors came there, all the people looking for other survivors, with a picture in their hand, a photograph, a letter, a something, asking people, 'Do you know this person? You saw him? You know what happened? You know someone who does? Maybe you can help? Maybe you can find out?'" My mother had told me that she also went to Place Rouppe daily, looking for information about my father. However, that wasn't where she met Arnold; it was through Benjamin that Arnold found us.

"I met your uncle there who today lives in Israel," said Arnold, going on. "He told me about you and your mother. He was staying with her. He was in Auschwitz also.

"Anyway, I told Benjamin I had known his brother, and we talked for a long time. Then, as I had no place to stay, he told me I could stay where he was staying, with your mother, who would be glad to meet me and hear about her husband. So he took me to her, introduced me, and told her that I had been in camp with her husband, but that I didn't know what had happened to him after we had been separated. You were not there; your mother said that you were in an orphanage somewhere—I didn't quite understand why." My uncle Benjamin had been arrested as a teenager and deported to Auschwitz but had had the good fortune of being put to work in a sausage factory where desperate survival cleverness allowed him to smuggle some of the food out and later barter it advantageously with other inmates and even guards.

"After a while, Benjamin had to go out," Arnold went on. "I remembered that when night came he wasn't back yet. Maybe he found someone? Maybe he had a woman. He was still young. I don't know. Anyway, I was going to spend the night at your mother's apartment. She had those rooms on chaussée d'Etterbeek; I think she hid there during the war with an old couple who left as soon as the war was over.

"Your mother gave me the bedroom, and she was going to sleep in the other room. After I went to bed and your uncle wasn't back yet, Frau Katz moved all the furniture from the kitchen against the door—the table, the chairs, everything. I don't know what your mother thought I was going to do to her. She moved everything against the bedroom door." Remembering the big table and four wooden chairs we had in that apartment in Brussels and picturing my mother dragging it all across the room to block the door struck me as quite funny, but the twinkle in Arnold's eyes as he told me this reminded me that my mother had been very attractive as a young woman. Who knows?

"I knew your father was dead," he continued. "When I couldn't find him when I went back for him to put him on the train, I knew he was dead. They probably shot him, or something. I told your mother the story, but I couldn't convince her that her husband was dead, and, who knows, maybe a miracle had happened? Your mother went every day to Place Rouppe, looking for someone who had news about your father. Once, your mother told me, a man said that he had heard something about your father, that he had heard that Katz was living in Munich with another woman. I don't think your mother believed him, but maybe she believed him ten percent. Your father never would have done that, not coming back to his wife and child in Belgium, but she believed that man ten percent." These words stirred memories of suspicions that I had had as a child, knowing that since some people had come back from concentration camps, I sometimes thought that my father had abandoned us, that he was living somewhere with another wife and child, and I had felt both great anger and pain at this possibility.

"After a while," continued Arnold, "I got my own place in Brussels, and I started a business that took me back to Germany. I met and married Helen there, and we came back later to live in Brussels.

"You look just like your father. Exactly. He was full of jokes in camp. Always. *Vitzler*—joker. You know one time I got really angry with him. It was toward the end. The Allies were dropping bombs all over. Before we went out into the fields to work, the bombs had to be unearthed, defused. They called for volunteers: you didn't have to go, you know. They would give you an extra piece of bread for it, just a piece of bread. You have to understand what that meant to us, that extra piece of bread.

"Your father volunteered. I was very angry at him when I found out. I could have killed him. I told him, 'You're crazy, you are going to go, and for what? You could die.' But he went and worked all day, looking for bombs. Nothing happened, thank God. At one point the volunteers were all in the pit, a pit where there was a bomb. They all went inside the pit, but the Germans stayed outside, up on the top, watching. Your father handled the bomb, then looked up at the Germans and said: 'It is written here, "This bomb won't hurt Jews, only Germans."' Everybody laughed. The Germans didn't do anything to him. They could have killed him, but they didn't. Life wasn't so bad."

As Arnold was telling me this story, it occurred to me, for a brief moment, that the dead man from Belgium in the camp whose identity he had appropriated might have been my father's. And then I thought about his saying at first that he had been in Buchenwald. Had he really known my father in the camp and carried him on his back? If that wasn't true, why had he come to Belgium to look us up, and why his attachment to us? And why sponsor us to come to America? Guilt on his part? Even though it was thanks to him that we were able to leave Belgium, my mother always distrusted Arnold but could never articulate her reasons, perhaps because he had survived and my father hadn't. Maybe I was repeating my mother's mistrust. Not really, but perhaps ten percent, as Arnold would say.

CONCLUSION

Arnold told me many other stories about himself in Auschwitz that afternoon, but I could barely concentrate on them. I kept going back to the picture of my father, an old man at the age of thirty-five, lying on the cold, snowy ground somewhere in the woods of Poland that January 1945. Did another German soldier stand over him and pull out his pistol, this time with no one to stop him from shooting? Or did my father drag himself somewhere else, trying to find out what was happening in the chaos and not waiting for Arnold to return? Perhaps he had gotten on a train without Arnold and died in his seat? Or did he simply die of cold where he lay?

I will never know. I did not want this image of my father's vulnerability to be the lasting one in my mind, and yet it was more compelling than the one of him as a young man playing with me, carrying me on his shoulders. No stories about his own childhood in Czechoslovakia have survived. I knew nothing about his adolescence or about his years as a young bachelor in Antwerp; what little I knew about him was secondhand. According to my mother, he was "irresponsible." My twice-removed cousin Max—Henna Wunderman's oldest son, who as a child had known him as a married man in Antwerp—remembered his sense of humor and his love of adventure. From his younger brother, my uncle Benjamin, I had a picture of my father as a romantic who courted my mother against his own father's wishes. The truth is that finding out how he died would not have revealed what kind of man he had been; Arnold's stories had not helped. Instead, the documents in his file in Brussels had been the most concrete evidence of his existence. The official recording of his arrest, his German identification card, his concentration camp number—all these remnants of his suffering had been the most help in re-creating his reality. How ironic that he had been so present for me in his documented absence. Reading those papers had been a little like being able to hug him; I was touched by the proof that he had really existed and that he had been my father. There are no photographs of us together, no letters from him addressed to me, no toys that he must have bought me; all I had of him were those papers in his file.

Although I had put much stock in the few stories I had been told, especially those of his love of children and also of his special feelings toward me, they were too general, too bland to draw a convincing portrait. My mother's faded memories were too subjective to evoke him for me, and, besides, those memories were over forty years old. I even wondered how well my parents had known each other. They had been married only four years when my father disappeared; four years of intimacy during horrific and dangerous times when most decisions had life-changing consequences on one's resolve to survive and protect the people one loved.

I think time had sifted out feelings of affection and tenderness that my mother once had toward my father, but had kept alive her resentment and lingering anger because he had refused to listen to her when she begged him not to go to the meeting that led to his arrest. She had warned him that it was too dangerous to try to save his brother, and she had been proven right. She couldn't really answer my questions. I realize that I would never find out what he had been like, and that had really been the purpose of my search; I had wanted to connect with the particular man, the individual being who had been my father. I had failed! But perhaps that search was doomed from the beginning. What is left of a man after he disappears? Photos, letters, diaries? Do these resurrect the person? After my wallet was stolen in Paris, all I had of him were three photographs: one taken to celebrate his engagement to my mother; one of them at their wedding, and a third photograph of the whole wedding party. To me, then, my father would always be a stranger.

I had not been much more successful at reconnecting with the family that had hidden me as a child during the war than I had been in resurrecting my father. In some ways, the Walschots had been more real to me than he was during my childhood, but nonetheless my memories were so vague that I did not completely trust them. Here again my mother was unable or unwilling to help me. Perhaps she had felt so guilty in giving me away to strangers, even though it was to save me, that she wanted to erase those years while I wanted to relive them.

When I met with Jeanne in Waterloo, I had found our reunion very moving, and yet it had not brought me the warmth and affection that I had hoped to find in it. For me, there was no way to connect that middle-aged woman with the teenager I had considered my sister during the war. And how could she have seen her little "Astrid" in the American woman who seemed so uncomfortable in her home? Even the time we had shared the same house was remembered by us very differently. No matter how happy I had been with her family, I could not have forgotten that I had a big secret and that Mama Gine was not my real mother; there must have been underlying feelings of danger and confusion over divided loyalties, no matter how carefree my childish behavior appeared. I remember having many nightmares then, and I remember how I had clung to Papa Franz, needing to be loved by a man who could replace my absent father.

I owed Jeanne's family a debt I could never repay; they had saved my life. The Walschots had been "righteous people," in that they had been willing to take in a Jewish child they had never met and to raise her as their daughter. The danger was immense, yet I don't remember their ever being fearful. Why did they do it? Neither Martin nor Jeanne knew. Perhaps Papa Franz and Mama Gine would have been unable to explain the reason for the risks they had taken except to say, as the people in the film *As If It Were Yesterday* said, that it wasn't right, "you don't let children be killed." Had they still been alive, would our reunion have been different? Would I ever have been able to repay them?

Maybe I had waited too long to find them, and by the time I began my search, I took my survival for granted; I no longer thought of my life as a debt I owed that family. Perhaps it was my feeling of ingratitude that prevented me from connecting to Jeanne, who even as an adult had been so sweet to me. It wasn't so much that we had little in common now. She had spent all her life near Beersel, the village she was born in, and had gotten married young to a local boy; her life had followed a trajectory so unlike that of mine. But more than that, I think what created the distance between us was the realization that the war years had been different for her because she wasn't Jewish. Her family's courageous actions had been a choice, not a necessity. This made her family heroic, but it was a choice that my family never had had.

While Belgium was occupied and its citizens suffered many hardships, only the Jews had been marked for extinction. In spite of the established police state, the others could lead a sort of normal life under difficult conditions. There had been no normalcy for my family. Although I was not conscious of it at the time of my visit to Belgium forty years after the war, in retrospect, as I write this, I think my discomfort at the country's flourishing, my feeling that the war had been erased, was further realization that life had been so different for Jews and non-Jews during those years. After the war many Belgians had been able to pick up the pieces, rebuild, and prosper, but my family had been destroyed; all its members except my mother, Henna, her husband and three children, and one uncle had been pulled from Belgium and murdered in the camps of Poland and Germany. I would never feel at home in a country whose fate had been so different from mine; the desecration of the Jewish Memorial at the time of my visit had revived memories of anti-Semitic danger. While for me Belgium brought up memories of disappearances, danger, and separation, the country itself showed signs of its riches everywhere: the skyscrapers were full of prosperous businesses, successful American companies dotted the landscape, and there were prestigious universities, convenient fast-food restaurants, gleaming hotels . . .

It was irrational for me to begrudge Belgium its well-being, but I couldn't help feeling excluded and like a foreigner in the country of my birth. For all my discoveries there, my past was erased. I would never reconnect to my childhood; all those grandparents, uncles, aunts, cousins who had shared it would always be strangers. The Walschots would remain just as unknown to me as were my blood relatives.

I could not have explained all that to my mother when we met after I returned from my trips to Belgium. I told her of going to Beersel and seeing the Walschot house, of visiting Martin, and of meeting Jeanne in Waterloo. She listened quietly to what I had to say, then asked: "Is Jeanne as fat as her mother was?" I was flabbergasted; after all that I had told her, I expected questions and comments about how interesting it had all been and some curiosity about the events I had described. I hadn't expected such an irrelevant, cutting remark. I asked what she meant. "Well," she said, "Madame Walschot had been fat." That was true, but it wasn't what came to my mind when I thought of her.

"How do you know?" I asked. "When did you ever meet her?"

"When I came to take you home. Believe me, she was glad to see you go," she added. Since I had absolutely no memory of our reunion then, I couldn't contradict her, but I told her that was not the impression either Jeanne or Martin had given me. "Of course not," she said, and told me I didn't understand what had been going on. If their life had been in danger, they would have given me up. She insisted that they had agreed to hide me for the money the resistance paid them. These were the same remarks she had made before my trip. And besides, she added, Martin Walschot had made passes at her when she came to his shop to see me.

"Do you have any idea how that made me feel?" she asked. "I was so afraid that by turning him down, I would make him angry and he would take it out on you, maybe turn you in. I was so worried about you all the time."

From what I had learned on my trip, I thought her worries had been needless; I just couldn't see how they would have behaved that way, but by now I almost understand her feelings. She had been in Brussels by herself after giving me away and had lived through the disappearance of so many of her relatives and friends, some of them betrayed by neighbors or acquaintances. She had no one left to turn to besides Henna, and for a long time she did not know how I was faring. It was not surprising that she was suspicious of non-Jews, even of the family that was hiding me.

When I told her about reading the files at the Ministry of Public Health and learning what happened to my father after his arrest, she listened quietly and just said, "Poor man." I didn't tell her of my visit to La Hulpe; I didn't see the point of it. I had asked her many times why she had placed and left me there for so long; she was always so evasive that I knew she would never tell me the true story—true for me but perhaps not for her. What had her life been like without me those years? Did she have a new man and was afraid to test his devotion by saddling him with a seven-year-old? Was it Landau? She had denied these suppositions in the past, and I knew she would deny them again if I brought up my visit and asked the same questions.

When I came to Los Angeles after my visit with Arnold in San Francisco, I told my mother about our encounter. She asked why I had gone to see him, and when I told her that it was to find out how my father died, she just shrugged her shoulders.

"After so many years, what difference does it make? And besides, who knows if he would tell you the truth?" Then she asked about Louise, his new wife. Was she as nice as Helen? Now that Helen was dead, my mother was full of praise for her. I knew that our memory of the war years would never be the same, and although I have stuck to my own interpretation, I wonder if her attitude had not been a stronger influence than I realized at the time. Perhaps her own negative feelings made me so ambivalent about reconnecting emotionally with Jeanne. The discomfort I had felt might have also been due to a certain disloyalty I didn't want to feel toward my mother. Did I hold back my emotions because of it? I had sensed that Jeanne wanted little Astrid back, and I didn't want to be Astrid anymore. I had wanted to recapture my childhood, but I did not want to be recaptured by it.

We never talked about these trips again, neither when I visited her in her apartment nor when I saw her in the assisted-living home I placed her into when she was eighty-six. By then she was no longer able to live alone in her walk-up; she had fallen several times, left the stove burners on, became confused on the once-familiar streets. Assisted living was the only solution, but she hated the home as much as I had hated La Hulpe. I think she waited for my visits as eagerly as I had waited for hers, and just as I had been a difficult child, she was a difficult resident. Whenever I came to see her, I had to soothe several people, other residents or staff members, who complained about her behavior—"L'Enfant Terrible," in the words of the director.

I waited forty years to go back to Belgium to reconnect with my childhood, and I waited several decades to write about the experience. It was only as my mother was approaching the end of her life that I began to feel an overwhelming need to tell these stories. By then, I had been taking notes whenever she started talking again about the past, but I felt I couldn't really write this book while she was still alive. I knew she would not have liked the way I portrayed the people she remembered, and I couldn't have written about her baldness without feeling I was betraying her secret. For a long time, I was afraid people would find out I was Jewish; for her whole life, my mother was afraid that people would find out she wore a wig. Yet I had to include that fact in her story; it had played such a major role in her life. While a great impediment to her self-esteem, I think it accounted for her nonconformity—a trait that served her well during the war but poorly in the end when she chafed against the rules of the assisted-living home.

My mother's English and reading ability would not have been sufficient to read my book, but she would have known people who could read it and tell her about it, and I think she would have been mortified. But perhaps another reason I didn't write sooner is that I thought I didn't remember enough of those years to be able to tell about them. I know that you can't force memory; it doesn't come by consciously concentrating and trying hard to conjure images. But when the need to write overcame my lack of confidence, I found that in the very act of putting things down on paper, doors opened to rooms I didn't know existed, even if at times only ajar, but enough for me to reconstruct lives.

As I write this, almost everyone mentioned in this book, including my mother, is dead, and I have lost touch with Jeanne and Martin. I know that some questions will never be answered, but having found the strangers I was looking for, I can now start putting them to rest.

ACKNOWLEDGMENTS

I wish to express my deepest gratitude to the Walschot family for saving my life by hiding me during World War II. Chances are that without them I would not have been around to write this book. I am thankful to Myriam Abramowicz and Esther Hoffenberg for their 1980 documentary, *Comme ci c'était hier* (*As If It Were Yesterday*). Their film and their encouragement made my search possible. They also gave me a place to stay in Brussels during that difficult weekend in 1982. I am also most grateful to Richard Kenigsman for being my friend and acting as my chauffeur by driving me from Brussels to Beersel and La Hulpe when I was looking for people and institutions. I am very indebted to Berel Lang for his careful reading of this book; his counsel and advice were invaluable. Hettie Jones's encouragement was appreciated, as were the suggestions of Jane Roseman and Patricia Mulcaney. Ina Lancman and Nancy Salz read various drafts of my manuscript and were most helpful with their suggestions; they encouraged me to dig deeper. My friend Phyllis Bellano has been a fan of my writing since high school, and I am grateful for her support as well as that of Susan Dunn, who encouraged me to seek a publisher early on.

I also wish to express my gratitude to my wonderful editor,

T. David Brent, whose encouragement and insightful reading of my manuscript revealed gaps I hadn't noticed and was able to fill. And most of all, I want to thank my lucky stars for giving me Andy, a loving husband who throughout the time it took to write this book was most patient when patience was needed.